FROM HELIGOLAND TO HEAVEN
IN FIVE YEARS

PETER DONALDSON

Published by

MELROSE BOOKS

An Imprint of Melrose Press Limited
St Thomas Place, Ely
Cambridgeshire
CB7 4GG, UK
www.melrosebooks.com

FIRST EDITION

Cover designed by Peter Donaldson

ISBN 978 1 906561 11 6

Printed and bound in Great Britain by:
CPI Antony Rowe, Chippenham, Wiltshire

I dedicate this book to my late wife Nancy,
who throughout our sixty years of marriage
encouraged all my literary endeavours.

I wish to thank all the members of my wider family
for their support during the writing of the book.
In particular I thank my daughter Diana, whose encouragement and advice were invaluable.

The typing and editing of the manuscript
were services provided by Sharon Vaillant.
I am indebted to her.

CONTENTS

INTRODUCTION

Readers may find it strange that I am able to recall events that occurred about sixty-eight years ago. I will explain. On returning to England in 1945, I wrote an account of my war experiences for circulation to members of my family and I kept several copies on file.

In 1980 I retired from the headship of a state school, following increasing governmental interference in the conduct of the school. At the tender age of sixty I now had the time to write an autobiography which spanned my whole life at that time. The section dealing with the war years was used extensively when writing the present book.

My memory has been stimulated by the talks which I have given to groups interested in the veterans who served in the Second World War.

FROM HELIGOLAND TO
HEAVEN IN FIVE YEARS

I was eighteen when I commenced training as a navigator, bomb aimer and air gunner, at the Flying Training School in Yatesbury, situated below one of Wiltshire's white horses – a useful landmark for nervous navigators. On March 23rd 1939 I made my first flight in an Avro Anson, piloted by a Flight Lieutenant Lucke. I hoped this was a good omen. The small-cabined plane was very manoeuvrable, and had my pilot not been so named, I would have found the steep turns and sideslips a terrifying introduction to air travel. As it was, I just felt mildly apprehensive, sitting at the navigation table watching the patchwork of fields swing crazily about my head and feeling the bulk of my parachute stowed reassuringly close by.

As the weeks went by, I gradually learnt the theory and practice of dead reckoning navigation. Pinpointing specific features of the landscape below was essential if an accurate calculation of wind speed and direction was to be made. No electronic aids were available – in fact the only aid was a hand-held compass which was used to calculate drift.

I flew with Flight Lieutenant Lucke for most of my training. The

Westland Wallace, 1939

poor man seemed to suffer from a weak bladder and as the plane had no toilet facilities, the small cabin which we shared would slowly take on the aroma of a neglected public urinal; but his experience as a pilot was ample compensation for this slight inconvenience.

One of the most interesting exercises was called interception. This involved navigating the Anson to intercept another aircraft which had taken off at a pre-arranged time from a base some hundred miles away. (Fine weather was essential for this hazardous undertaking.) It was always a great thrill to see one's target ahead for it meant that you had got your sums right.

The navigation course at Yatesbury finished in June, amidst rumours of war. The trainees invaded the local pub and there was much singing of unmentionable ditties before we all staggered back to our billets. War was far from our minds.

Some – including myself – countered the inevitable hangover by running up the hill to the White Horse before returning for a shower and light breakfast. Jack Davis, my particular friend, had spent a dreadful night watching his room rotating about his head between periodic bouts of sickness. He was a stocky fellow from rural Gloucestershire – more familiar with cider than Wiltshire ale. He had great difficulty getting out of bed and no amount of urging from me would persuade him to tackle the White Horse. I covered up for him on the last day. He wasn't around to hear one of the instructors say to a colleague, 'Most of these poor buggers will bite the dust during the first week of a war.'

For the next part of my training, I was sent to the No. 1 Air Observer School at North Coates in Lincolnshire.

Here, during the months of July and August, we were to be trained in the use of machine-guns and bombsights, using aircraft that looked like leftovers from the 1914–18 war. These Westland Wallaces were biplanes with two open cockpits and a radial engine powering a huge propeller which had been designed to give them an increased ceiling: they were, in fact, the first air-

Avro Anson used for navigational training 1939

craft to fly over the summit of Mount Everest.

Not only were they ancient but they were equipped with obsolete Lewis machine-guns – noted for their frequent stoppages – and bomb-release mechanisms which would have done justice to Heath Robinson. None of this, however, diminished the intoxication which we experienced flying in these old machines. They bumped and shuddered over the coarse grass airfield during take-off and, once aloft, they played a concerto on the strut wires and the protruding barrel of the machine-gun. The straps of your flying helmet flapped and you flapped yourself if your gun jammed and your tool-kit was whipped out of your hand by the slipstream.

Walter Coveney, a slender, gaunt-faced lad from the London area, had become friends with Jack Davis and myself. We formed an inseparable trio for the remainder of the training course, a friendship which continued after we had qualified, as we were all posted to the same squadron. At first I thought this was a happy coincidence, but much later I realised that our surnames were in alphabetical order. Fate, working through an unknown administrative clerk, had already decided who was going to live and who was going to die. In the event of war, being posted to a front-line bomber squadron would, of course, diminish our chances of survival.

But our training was not yet finished and Walter was having trouble swinging the Lewis gun against the slipstream to shoot at targets lined up on the beach. One day, determined to succeed, he put his whole weight behind the gun, which pivoted through a wide arc to clout his unfortunate pilot in the front cockpit. He slumped forward and the plane dropped several hundred feet before it was brought under control. Had the pilot not been wearing a helmet, the result might have been unpleasantly different.

My own attempts to master air-to-ground firing were not without blemish. It had been impressed on the trainees that machine-guns must never – repeat never – be pointed in a landward direction. This meant that the mounting had to be rotated through 180 degrees whenever the pilot turned to make another run at the target.

In a moment of forgetfulness, I left the gun pointing in the forbidden direction. Realising my mistake, I hurriedly grabbed at it. A single dull report told me that a round was on its way across the fields towards a distant cowshed.

Luckily for me, the pilot didn't report the incident, and as neither human nor bovine casualties were notified to the school, I assumed with relief that the errant bullet had gone harmlessly to ground.

Dropping the practice bombs seemed great fun – rather like a fairground game. The missiles were small and harmless enough, unless you scored a direct hit on some unfortunate airman detailed to plot the smoke plumes from the fragile safety of a sighting hut at the perimeter of the beach range. The authorities obviously recognised the perilous nature of this duty by granting double pay to all concerned.

The tangle of pulleys and wires which formed the release mechanism was very unreliable. There were frequent hang-ups and – even worse – partial hang-ups when bombs would fall off at random at any time between take-off and landing. The best result I achieved was hitting a point 200 yards from the target from a height of 6,000 feet. It did occur to many of us that if we ever went to war against Adolf Hitler, his cardboard tanks would be in no peril from the Royal Air Force.

A brief – but not brief enough – spell of square-bashing at Uxbridge had been arranged to instil some service discipline into the trainees before they were dispersed to various squadrons. Not wishing to fall foul of the drill instructors, I thought it prudent to pay a prompt visit to the station barber. No sooner had I emerged with a bare inch of bristle beneath my forage cap when a flight sergeant stopped me in my tracks.

'Get your hair cut, airman!' he roared as if my hearing was impaired.

'Yes,' I replied meekly.

'Now listen, airman, you may be getting your stripes up in a few weeks' time like all the bloody observers, but until that happy day you will address me as flight sergeant. Is that understood?'

'Yes, flight sergeant.'

'And another thing – the next time I call you, don't saunter up to me like I was yer mother. You're in the Air Force now. When I say come 'ere, you don't walk, you don't run, you flyeeee … Understand?'

'Yes, flight sergeant.'

Four weeks of physical education and drill, interspersed with cold showers and lectures on Air Force history gave me a glow of health which I had not experienced since leaving school. However, my knowledge of Air Force history remained minimal as I usually fell asleep during the afternoon lectures – exhausted by the harshness of the morning's physical routine.

The worst part was gas drill. P.E. sessions were demanding enough without having one's face enclosed in a thick rubber mask: just about tolerable on a cold day, but in the hot June of 1939 it took its toll. I managed to keep upright, but the memory of the sweat and the hut full of tear gas remains with me to this day.

Before leaving Uxbridge, I managed a weekend at home. Mother could not hide her disappointment on seeing my convict-like appearance. She obviously had not read the small print and had expected me to be wearing a tailor-cut uniform complete with wings. All I could display was a rather tatty propeller – the arm badge of a leading airman – on a coarse, ill-fitting tunic.

So I came to the end of my initial training, passing out in the top third of the intake. Only in aerial photography were my results bordering on failure: nothing seemed to go right for me in that department, for I either had the ground out of focus or the timing wrong – once I even forgot to load the film.

Another reason for failing the photography course was my spell in Yatesbury R.A.F. hospital, following a blood test which revealed that I was suffering from arsenic poisoning. Nobody was deliberately trying to bump me off! It was caused by many months of handling telephone cables at the International Telephone Exchange in London. The cables were treated with arsenic to kill rats – nobody in authority had realised that arsenic could also kill humans!

The travel warrant informed me that my destination was R.A.F. Dishforth in Yorkshire. My orders were to report to Squadron Leader Whitworth, officer commanding 'B' flight, 10 Squadron. (It was August 1939 and the outbreak of war was barely a month away.)

I met up with Jack Davis and Walter Coveney en route to the Melmerby railway stop, near Ripon, where an R.A.F. transport was waiting to take the three of us on the last few miles of our journey along country roads that twisted through a landscape lush with fields of green and yellow ochre. This was my first visit to

Yorkshire. The impression of bright sun shimmering on the corn and the distant Hambleton hills beyond stayed with me over the years yet to come.

Our reception in the sergeants' mess was cool. Most of the N.C.O.s had taken many years of service to win their stripes and they looked upon this new breed of direct-entry observers with some disdain. The senior station warrant officer watched us closely for any breach of mess rules and pounced on me for removing my jacket when playing a game of table tennis in the recreation room. We all felt rejected. We spent many hours lazing in the sun outside 'B' flight hangar, watching the coffin-shaped Whitleys take off and land. Our navigational skills were not required, and we were only used as ballast when a pilot wanted a passenger in the rear turret to assist in keeping the aircraft in trim. At other times we crawled about the cabins of grounded bombers, trying to fathom the workings of unfamiliar guns and bombsights.

Sometimes, huddled in a corner of the mess, we spoke about our training or – to be more precise – our lack of it. None of us had more than fifty hours' flying to his credit; of this total only six had been logged at night. Yet here we were, grounded beneath a cloudless sky.

Pilots, wireless operators and gunners had been able to make good use of the August weather, with frequent training flights over the Yorkshire Dales and beyond; but it seemed that Wing Commander 'Crack 'Em' Staton, the Officer Commanding 10 Squadron, did not wish to trust his bombers to the inexperienced, half-trained observers whom the Air Ministry had dumped on him. Navigation and bomb-aiming had always been the prerogative of the second pilot, who had also been trained to use the Vickers gun in the front turret. If observers were to take over these duties, second pilots would be relegated to sit in the well by the forward hatch and fly when called upon by the skipper. Not a very promising prospect for them.

Another grievance which we aired amongst ourselves was our complete ignorance of the workings of either the Vickers or the Browning machine-guns. The Lewis gun with which we had so valiantly struggled in the old Westland Wallaces had not been used on the squadron for several years. If anybody needed additional training, it was certainly us.

We were in the Mess on Sunday, September 3rd and heard the Downing Street broadcast. Chamberlain sounded dispirited. The news that we were now at a state of war with Germany was greeted in silence; slowly the room emptied as people dispersed to ponder the significance of the news in the privacy of their billets. A distant air-raid siren wailed, to be followed almost immediately by an 'all clear'.

My own feelings were a mixture of exhilaration and apprehension. The possibility of death gnawed at the edges of my mind. Would we be sent half-trained into battle? How would the sluggish old Whitleys stand up to the German fighters? Would we be able to navigate in the dark when most of our experience had been based on daylight pin-pointing?

The Air Ministry was in no doubt. Within a few weeks all the squadron observers were sent to St Athan on an astronavigation course with a view to teaching us how to use a sextant and take bearings on the stars. It rained for most of the fortnight and all I could log was six and a half hours of daylight flying. There wasn't a star in sight, only an occasional glimpse of the moon and Venus low on the horizon. The waterlogged and corrugated wings of the Ansons, for which St Athan had no hangar space, looked unsafe and we were all glad to return safely to Dishforth.

Wing Commander Staton (who finished his R.A.F. career as an Air Vice Marshal) was now resigned to employing the observers in the capacity for which they had been intended by the Ministry. For reasons best known to him, he chose me as his navigator – a decision which he was later to regret.

My first operational trip began at three p.m. on December 17th 1939. Our orders were to drop leaflets over the Bremen area: a dull, unrewarding activity which was heightened by throwing out untied bundles, accompanied by occasional empty beer bottles (which we believed would whine like real bombs) in the forlorn hope that we would give some unsuspecting Nazi a nasty headache.

'Crack 'Em' didn't worry about the searchlights which illuminated the cabin from time to time. Neither did he seem to care a jot for the bursts of flak which buffeted us about on our return journey – as an ex-First World War fighter pilot, he seemed to think the present operation was rather tame. The fact that he never took evasive action made my job as navigator much easier and we returned to Dishforth at eleven pm. without any problems. I had handed frequent alterations of course to 'Crack 'Em' but I landed with the distinct impression that he would have reached base without any help from me.

Now began three months of intensive training for the whole squadron. We were able to practise bomb-aiming and gunnery, and to take part in exercises with aircraft of Fighter Command. We also co-operated with ground defences in the Midlands by zig-zagging about the night sky, providing practice for our anti-aircraft gunners and searchlight units. It was during one of these exercises that I experienced the full blast of the C.O.'s ill temper – all his pent-up frustration against observers descended on my slender frame. It happened like this.

I was navigating him about the Leeds/Bradford area on an exercise with ground defences. He made frequent and sudden alterations of course, flinging the old Whitley about as if he were

Gunnery and Bombing training in Westland Wallace bi-plane

back over the trenches. After two hours of this evasive action, he brought the shuddering aircraft on to an even keel and asked me for a course to take us back to base. I made a quick calculation by the dimmed light over my navigation table and handed him the information.

Two minutes before E.T.A. (estimated time of arrival), he came down through the cloud, looking for the flare path. I was searching too, and all I could make out was the moonlit waters of the North Sea. At least, I hoped it was the North Sea and not the Irish Sea or the English Channel.

The outburst in my headphones was more frightening than the flak barrage I had experienced over Bremen. 'Second pilot,' he thundered, 'take over the navigation!'

With my future as a navigator in the balance, I sensed the situation demanded firm action.

'I got you into this mess, sir,' I shouted down the intercom. 'Let me get you out of it.'

Wing Commander Staton grunted.

'The second pilot cannot be expected to navigate from this er … er … doubtful position,' I added.

Another grunt seemed to indicate assent, so I handed him a reciprocal course and hoped for the best. Twenty minutes later, after I had pin-pointed a coastal steel furnace, the Whitley was bouncing happily down the Dishforth flare path.

The following morning, 'B' flight were gathered in the crew room to hear the C.O.'s assessment of the previous night's exercise.

'I don't know about your navigators, but mine got me lost,' he said. All heads turned in my direction. Jack Davis grinned and I rose slowly to my feet.

'I got you back, sir,' I said.

A ripple of laughter greeted my defence and no more was said

Gunnery trainees

of the matter.[1]

About this time the Air Ministry realised that Staton was too valuable to risk on further operations, so his crew were dispersed. Pilot Officer Warren, the C.O.'s second pilot, was given his own aircraft and I became his navigator. But nobody was going to tie 'Crack 'Em' down to a desk without a fight. On the night of March 19th 1940, he persuaded the authorities to let him take part in a raid on the seaplane base on Sylt. For leading this operation he was awarded the D.S.O. and I felt proud to have navigated him there – and back – without any hitches. Whether the raid achieved anything is another matter, for reconnaissance photographs showed that, in spite of the large number of bombers deployed, the seaplane base was undamaged. (Later in the war I met a German soldier who was stationed on the island at the time of the raid. He reported that most of the bombs had fallen in the sea and that the only casualty on the island was a rabbit!) I received a letter from Mother, who told me she had been to the cinema and seen me on the Pathé news describing the raid on Sylt. She stood up, shouting, 'That's my son!'

As the winter increased in severity, so the squadron casualties started to mount. The intense cold penetrated our flying suits, our gloves and fur-lined boots. It caused icing on the wings with a consequent serious loss of performance. More significantly the cold seemed to generate a mental torpor in the five members of the crew, denying us that alertness which was essential for survival. Perhaps it was this last factor which caused Walter's death

---

1 The cause of this debacle was an administrative failure by the person responsible for updating the signals on the nationwide flashing beacons. In 1940 these were situated close to air bases. They were activated during hours of darkness and flashed Morse code signals which were changed every 24 hours. In order to be well prepared for Staton's exercise with our ground defences, I visited the crew room early to copy the codes from the blackboard. Later I discovered that I had copied the codes from the previous day. These should have been erased by the officer responsible. Later in the year all the beacons were withdrawn from service.

when his Whitley crashed into the Pennines, instantly killing him and two other members of the crew.

Poor Walter. He had fallen in love with a Ripon girl. He seemed to sense that his time was running out, for he had curbed his natural shyness to hasten the affair along. A few days before the crash, I had joined him to make a foursome for dinner at the Unicorn Hotel in Ripon. Half-way through the meal, Walter's girlfriend

Above and right:
Author, 1940

turned to him and said, 'What are you thinking about, Walter?'

Walter smiled sheepishly and, looking straight at the fair, young questioner, he replied, 'I was thinking how nice it would be to make love to you.'

Like so many young aircrew, he died before he could consummate his love.

I got three days' leave after the raid on Sylt, and took a train to London. The city was blacked out and the taxi which took me home had its headlights reduced to two small slits. There were air-raid wardens on nearly every street corner – I met one brandishing a carving knife which, he informed me, was intended for any German parachutist who came within sight.

Mother had started a boarding house in Kensington. It was a short-lived enterprise, as the Blitz was only a few weeks away. In the meantime, her chief enemy was a lodger who swore at her and refused to pay his account. A telephone call to my brother Stewart (still in the police force) worked wonders: the sight of his uniform and the sound of his deep, commanding voice had the man's wallet out in quick time, followed by a hasty retreat into the night.

RAF Dishforth Winter 1940

Returning to Dishforth, I saw three crashed Whitleys at crazy angles on the perimeter of the airfield. One was perforated with shrapnel but the other two had fallen foul of the atrocious weather.

Spring brought hope for better things to come. Soon we were flying again without being encased in layers of heavy clothing, and we could start our operations in daylight – a positive advantage for dead reckoning navigation. But pressure on the squadron increased when Hitler pushed his forces into Norway.

I was now firmly established as Pilot Officer Warren's navigator and we successfully completed ten operations in April and May. One of these targets was the airfield at Stavanger. It is doubtful if our bombs had much effect, as the base was constructed on solid rock, but we might have made a few dents on the runway.

On the return flight, we were diverted to Leuchars near Dundee, as Dishforth was fogbound. Everything seemed to be going along well. I checked and re-checked our course and then did something which I had always dreaded on night trips: I fell asleep at my navigation table.

I awoke with Warren's voice in my headphone asking me for an E.T.A. I couldn't believe my watch, which told me that I had been out for nearly an hour, until I saw dawn beginning to light up the cloud bank below. The wireless operator got me a loop bearing on a radio beacon and I calculated our position at about 90 miles from the Scottish coast. The cloud thinned enough to reveal the sea below, but when my E.T.A. expired, the coast was nowhere to be seen. I was starting to get worried when the second pilot, seated behind the Vickers gun in the front turret, shouted, 'Land ahead!'

Half an hour later we touched down at Leuchars in the teeth of a westerly gale which accounted for our loss of speed on the homeward journey.

After breakfast in the sergeants' mess, the crew had a brief snooze before taking a taxi into Dundee. Still in our flying gear, we headed for a licensed restaurant. To our amazement several diners stood up and clapped us as we took our seats. We felt – and no doubt looked – embarrassed at this spontaneous display of encouragement. There was little to cheer about in the Spring of 1940 – our army was bogged down behind the Maginot Line and the Navy had not engaged the enemy in any significant way, but at least the Air Force was hitting back.

On May 10th, the Germans invaded the Low Countries and, at the same time, made a powerful armoured thrust through the Ardennes, taking the French completely by surprise. By the end of the month, the blitzkrieg had achieved all its targets, which included trapping the entire British Expeditionary Force around Dunkirk. These swift, catastrophic events bore down heavily on the crews of 10 Squadron, who were given targets in support of the retreating Allied armies.

On May 27th, we took off from Dishforth to attack a Luftwaffe base in Holland. What happened during the next eight hours has since passed into R.A.F. history.

The weather was fair over the North York Moors, but as we cleared Flamborough Head we were confronted by a large storm cloud across our intended track. It was nine p.m. and darkness was beginning to close in. As soon as we entered the voluminous grey mass, lightning flashed between the gun barrels and the Whitley shuddered in protest. Warren attempted to climb out of trouble, and this he succeeded in doing after several alterations of course.

Although we were out of the cloud, visibility was still poor and I asked Rattigan, the second pilot, to keep a sharp look-out for the Dutch coast from his position of vantage in the front turret. Pin-pointing was difficult, but after about an hour, searchlights stabbed the darkness ahead and an estuary came into view.

The flak barrage which followed was the heaviest I had experienced – the shrapnel thudding into the bomb doors beneath my feet did little to sustain my concentration on matters navigational.

Rattigan reported an airfield ahead, so Warren put the Whitley into a shallow dive to take a closer look. It seemed to be just what we were looking for, and as our E.T.A. had expired there was little point in stooging around any longer. To avoid all the hassle of changing places, it was agreed that Rattigan should do the bomb-aiming.

Soon an excited cry down the intercom informed the crew that our 500-lb bombs had scored a direct hit on the runway. Now we veered away and headed for home.

A straight line connecting the Dutch airfield with Dishforth passes north-east of the Wash. Imagine my astonishment, therefore, when we were intercepted by two Spitfires over Liverpool – there was no mistaking the docks for it was now almost daylight. The fighters took a good look at us before deciding that we were genuine friends who had gone somewhat astray.

With deep misgivings, I handed the skipper a course for base, which we reached without incident half an hour later.

I clambered out of the forward hatch, gripping my parachute, charts and log book, and walked awkwardly with Warren towards the crew room. Suddenly he stopped and grasped my arm. 'You realise that we have dropped our bombs in this country, don't you?' he said in a tired, toneless voice.

I nodded my agreement.

'For God's sake keep mum about it,' he added.

The crew trooped into the ops room for debriefing.

The intelligence officer's questions followed the usual pattern. How effective were the searchlights? What was the flak like? Any sign of enemy fighters? (No, just friendly, I was tempted to reply.)

We were about to leave when the questions I had dreaded most came floating quietly in my direction across the smoke-filled room. 'What time did you drop your bombs, navigator?'

I glanced quickly at Pilot Officer Warren, standing pale and erect, stroking his large ginger moustache. He shrugged his shoulders and I knew there was noway out.

'At half-past midnight,' I replied.

There was a moment of hesitation before the intelligence officer turned to a wall chart. Then a long pause before he spoke again. 'According to my information you gave Liverpool an air-raid warning at four a.m. this morning. If you dropped your bombs when you say you did, then you must have been flying at about three hundred miles per hour. Some speed for a Whitley, don't you think?'

We were concerned. The official cruising speed of a Mark V Whitley was 175 m.p.h., which it seldom achieved. Our ground speed on the return leg of the operation was less than 150 m.p.h. as we were flying into a 25 m.p.h. headwind.

The next and last question came like a rifle shot.

'Were the bombs dropped in this country?'

'I think so,' replied Warren, miserably.

A series of telephone calls to Fighter Command elucidated the information that R.A.F. Bassingbourn in Cambridgeshire had suffered an attack from an unidentified aircraft. A stick of bombs had made craters along the length of the runway.

'Were there any casualties?' cried Warren.

'Any casualties?' repeated the intelligence officer down the phone.

The whole crew waited for the verdict like the defendants in a dock searching the face of a jury foreman.

'None,' said the intelligence officer.

As expected, there was a full inquiry. My log book was scrutinised closely and the courses I had written on slips of paper were retrieved from the floor of the cabin. The compass was tested and found to be wildly inaccurate – evidently affected by the magnetic storm through which we had passed.

As skipper, Warren took the full blame, which was unfair but not surprising. The inquiry held him responsible for not relying more on his non-magnetic gyro compass following the magnetic storm. (An opinion easily arrived at in hindsight.) Doubtless, the squadron navigation officer, who conducted the inquiry, must have felt more sympathy for a fellow officer than for an N.C.O. But the irrefutable evidence of my log book could not be brushed away and I was completely exonerated, continuing as a navigator for another crew skippered by Flight Lieutenant Harrington. In the meantime Warren was demoted to second pilot.

It was a sad end to an excellent team. Warren had proved time and time again that he was an excellent pilot, showing unbelievable courage in the face of stiff enemy resistance. He was respected by every member of the crew.

Several developments followed – some amusing and some more serious.

Warren was nicknamed 'The Baron' by his fellow officers and was subjected to some ragging in the mess. A local fighter squadron sent a Spitfire to Dishforth and two cardboard Iron Crosses were deposited on the airfield.

A week or two later, I was on my way to prepare for another trip when I passed the open window of the billiards room of the sergeants' mess. 'Get airborne,' I shouted to my fellow airmen. 'Get Bassingbourn!' came a quick retort from one of the players.

In the meantime, Staton had flown to Bassingbourn to offer his personal apologies to the station commander. I wish I could have been a fly on the wall at that interview!

An examination of the craters brought a few raised eyebrows at the Air Ministry: they were far too small. The bombs we were using were old stock, probably stored since the First World War. An immediate order was issued to prohibit their use.

The final spin-off from what could have been a tragic disaster was the interest taken in the way that I had written up my log sheet, which was brought to the notice of those responsible for the training of observers. It became a model example of how to keep an accurate log, not only as an aid to navigation but as an essential document for safeguarding the reputation of navigators themselves. Four years later copies were still being distributed round lecture rooms.

I had always felt a great deal of respect for the German defences, but after the Bassingbourn incident, my respect for the British defences rose considerably. The flak barrage and search-lights which we had encountered on our run up to the 'target' had been directed at us with considerable accuracy by the gallant defenders stationed along the banks of the Thames estuary.

Some years ago, on visiting R.A.F. Leeming, I saw Flight Lieutenant Warren's name on the top of the Board of Honour at the entrance to the officers' mess. He had a D.F.C. after his name. I felt greatly cheered by this discovery.

With the fall of France, targets once again moved to the heart-land of Germany, and I took part in several raids over the Ruhr and to that much-bombed marshalling yard at Hamm.

On June 11th I got a new skipper, Flight Lieutenant Ffrench-Mullen. He was a fine pilot, utterly fearless and always consider-ate to his crew.

We had two fairly quiet operations before being handed a brief which looked ominously like a death warrant. Sergeant Miller, our wireless operator, met me in the mess when I returned from the briefing.

'You look worried,' he said. 'What's the target?'

'It's mines in the Rhine at Mannheim,' I replied, making a rather corny attempt to sound light-hearted. What I didn't tell him was that we would be expected to go in at low level to get accurate results, as the newly developed W mines we were carrying must in no circumstances be dropped on dry land where the enemy might defuse them and uncover their secrets. It seemed that the mines would only become active when they were immersed in water. (Later, several of them blew up near the bomb dump after a particularly heavy rain storm.) The aim of the enterprise was to destroy barges carrying vital oil supplies up the Rhine from the Rumanian wells.

I wrote a letter to my mother which was only to be sent in the event of my death. Then I went down to the armoury to withdraw a Colt .45 pistol and a clip of ammunition – a piece of personal insurance we had been recommended to include in our baggage.

The outward trip was uneventful, but things hotted up as we neared the target area. I crouched over the bombsight in the front turret, giving the pilot instructions over the intercom to bring the Whitley in line with the river gleaming in the pale moonlight. The enemy gunners on the hillsides soon got us in their sights, but we were so low that they were forced to fire downwards into the valley and put their own defences at risk. Then light flak opened up from the banks of the river and the sky around us danced with flashing lights.

I dropped a stick of mines and the rear gunner yelled that they had hit the water. Ffrench-Mullen turned to start another run – a necessary but, in my view, suicidal decision. I was wrong, for he came in so low and at such a speed that the defenders were unable to keep us in their sights. The mines went earthwards but it was impossible to see where they had landed on account of the frightening firework display over the river and the steep climb which the skipper had made to get us safely out of this valley of death.

I felt no strong feeling of obligation about making sure that the remaining mines were deposited in the Rhine. After 20 operations, my will to survive was gradually swamping the sense of duty which had motivated me during the early stages of the war. So I did not report to Ffrench-Mullen that a further run would be required to unload the remaining mines. Instead, I dropped them

23

as he turned the Whitley across the river further up the valley. They may have hit the water: if they missed, it was just too bad. As far as I was concerned, the top brass, sitting behind desks out of the firing line, could get stuffed!

We touched down at Dishforth after almost nine hours in the air, exhausted but thankful to be alive.

Whitley Mark 5 Bomber 10 Squad

The following morning I wandered down the hangar to inspect our Whitley. 'This is yours, sergeant!' called a fitter, handing me a lump of shrapnel which he had removed from the engine compartment. It had missed an oil feed pipe by barely two inches.

The fuselage had one or two perforations, but what surprised me most of all was the state of the wings, which had suffered large rents on the leading edge where the fabric had been shredded. This had not been caused directly by enemy action but by the high-speed dive which the skipper had initiated to escape from a searchlight cone and its associated flak barrage on our return flight.

More trips followed – some on consecutive nights, which gave us no time to rest our shattered nerves. Then came the trip which

Sergeant J Davis

was to alter my life – it was to be my last operation.

I suppose the strain was beginning to tell on me more than I cared to admit – even to myself. No excuse was needed for an outing to Harrogate or York, where one could unwind with the help of alcohol and one's aircrew buddies. It was after one such sally into the city taverns that I was brought home in a stupor, lying on the floor of a taxi at the feet of my revelling companions, reaching Dishforth after midnight. The mess bar was re-opened and I recovered enough to start another drinking session.

Hurdling over settees seemed great fun and I soon discovered that I could hurl myself at these obstacles without sustaining any apparent injuries. After one glorious flight, I landed in a heap and found that I could no longer haul myself to my feet. I lay paralysed on the beer-stained carpet, looking up at a circle of pulsating red faces until I felt myself being carried outside into the starlit night.

I remembered nothing until I was awakened by an orderly who informed me that the whole squadron was on the move to Leeming – a new R.A.F. station situated a few miles to the north of Dishforth.

In a state of shock, I pulled an old suitcase from under the bed to discover that a rodent of some sort had bored a large hole through my civilian clothes from top to bottom. I pushed it back again, packed my service kit and clambered aboard a truck with a helping hand from Jack Davis, who was sitting amongst the pile of kitbags looking disgustingly healthy. My head thumped, my bruised limbs ached and I felt ashamed of myself.

In the new mess at Leeming, I stared blankly at the cold ham salad in front of me. I couldn't believe it. I'd just been told that our crew had been picked for an operation to bomb the naval base at Kiel – take-off was scheduled for 2100 hours, which would give me just three hours to find a billet and make all the necessary flight preparations. My first reaction was to report sick immediately, but the thought was dismissed without consideration – sick notes were the hallmark of cowards, everybody knew that.

There is nothing like high altitude for clearing the brain. By the time we had reached 10,000 feet, heading due east over the North Sea, my head no longer ached and my stomach had responded well to a flask of N.A.A.F.I. coffee.

Low cloud covered the target area, so Ffrench-Mullen sent the second pilot into the front turret to pin-point a landmark through the occasional small breaks. We droned on westwards but saw nothing. At last, as we came near the point of no return, the skipper turned back for home with our bomb load intact. The whole operation seemed to have been a waste of time.

As we headed out over the North Sea again, the sky in the east slowly brightened and we began to lose the cloud cover which had enveloped us on the outward journey. Ffrench-Mullen was not only worried about the encroaching daylight but, even more so, he was worried about the fuel situation – we had used far too much looking for the elusive target. As I was still in the front turret, he ordered me to jettison the bombs and then return to my navigation table and concentrate on getting us back to base. I felt uneasy. It was now almost daylight and we were still within reach of the enemy. I put a pan of ammunition on the Vickers gun – just in case – before scrambling back into the cabin.

I had just plugged in my intercom when the excited voice of the rear gunner reported two fighters climbing steadily towards us from the distant coastline.

'I think they're Me 109s!' he shouted.

With my strong instinct for survival coming to the fore, I called Ffrench-Mullen without delay. 'Get down as low over the sea as you can, sir. They won't be able to come up underneath us if you do that.'

Ffrench-Mullen replied by putting the Whitley into a steep dive – perhaps his own survival instinct was as strong as my own.

Officers don't usually take orders from sergeants.

Our sudden tactic seemed to have momentarily frustrated the planned attack. Now the fighters levelled out and took up stations above and to the rear – one on each side just out of range of our guns. But we didn't have to wait long. They took it in turns to dive at us, firing tracer bullets which I could clearly see passing harmlessly ahead. They had obviously over-estimated the speed of the old Whitley.

I was a helpless spectator of a combat in which I no longer had a role to play. All I could do was to watch the tracer bullets come nearer and nearer until their lines of red dashes seemed to be coming straight at me, causing me to duck instinctively under the navigation table.

Now I could hear the rear gunner pumping away with the four Brownings and I could smell the cordite fumes wafting along the fuselage. 'I think I've got one!' he yelled.

I turned quickly in my seat, too frightened to respond to the cry of triumph for I had seen flames belching from the starboard engine – flames which were streaking along the surface of the trailing edge, devouring its fabric.

I could only see one fighter now. It turned and banked above the nose of the Whitley, exposing its belly to the second pilot, sitting behind the Vickers gun in the front turret.

'Hit him, man! Hit him!' I shouted, but the gun remained silent. (Later, I learnt that the second pilot had never had any instruction on how to fire the gun.)

Soon there were no fighters to be seen and for a brief moment I thought we were going to make it. Then the calm voice of Ffrench-Mullen sounded in my ears like a railway station announcer telling passengers that the four-thirty to Dishforth has been cancelled.

'Prepare to abandon aircraft!' he said firmly. I stumbled into the main fuselage where I was joined by the wireless operator, who told me he had screwed down his Morse key to send out a continuous distress signal. Without warning, the Whitley pan-caked on to the sea and we were both flung backwards to sprawl in a heap on the metal floor.

I scrambled to my feet, untied the dinghy and opened the main hatch. The sea that rushed in was green. Atkinson the rear gunner backed away from it – he couldn't swim. I pushed him in, having first made sure that his Mae West was inflated. Miller the wireless operator jumped in without any hesitation. I flung out the dinghy and followed.

The dinghy should have inflated automatically but it didn't.

'Swim over here with it, Donaldson.'

French-Mullen was standing over the water level on the port wing. I obeyed his instruction with some difficulty as my flying boots had filled with water. He bent down and turned the release valve on the compressed air bottle. The sound of the hissing air was like music to my ears.

Momentarily, I seemed to float away from the others, who were thrashing about in the ice-cold water waiting for the skip-per to complete his task. I'd blown too much air into my life jacket, making it buoyant enough to force me backwards. In this position, I was rocked by a gentle swell which gradually lulled away my fear, filling me with an intense feeling of elation. I started singing hysterically and with gusto, 'A Life on the Ocean Waves'. I had been reprieved. Providence had dismissed the fir-ing squad at the eleventh hour and I was overwhelmed by the joy of being alive.

I watched the rising sun send ripples of light to play on the doomed Whitley, which was slowly sinking amidst a sea of exploding bubbles, groaning and gurgling like a dying animal. It had carried us safely through many dangers but I was not sad to see it go – the flying coffin would not be claiming my body. In my joy, it never occurred to me that I was still in considerable peril – that even if I escaped death by drowning, the enemy might have unpleasant plans for dealing with British airmen.

The hissing had stopped. I lifted my head to see Ffrench-Mullen struggling, on the partly submerged wing, to upright the dinghy which had inflated in a capsized position. I swam over to give him a hand and together we managed to get it the right way up. Climbing into it was another matter. My limbs were numb and my waterlogged clothes were beginning to drag me down. With much heaving and grunting, many hands slowly pulled me in until I was floundering in the bottom like a fish out of water. Then I staggered wearily to my feet to join the rest of the crew, who were seated round the perimeter of our orange-coloured, air-filled lifesaver like characters from a nonsense poem. There was a feeling of unreality. Could this be happening to me? The shivering cold wetness and the sight of the Whitley just visible beneath the calm waters told me this was no dream. Not even the strange phosphorus beams glowing beneath the surface like underwater lights in a swimming pool could prolong my fantasy.

In silence, we watched bubbles rising from the depths as sea water seeped into the almost empty fuel tanks. Then there was nothing: no trace of the bomber, which would never fly again.

Ffrench-Mullen, who had stepped off the wing into the dinghy, was the only one of us who had not had a ducking. Now he pulled a packet of cigarettes from his tunic and handed them around.

'Did you see those fishing boats we passed over on the way down?' he said, addressing no one in particular.

'Yes,' replied the rear gunner, 'I gave them a short burst. We've been told that they radio our positions to the Jerries.'

Nobody commented – tact was never the rear gunner's strong point.

I was shaking badly now and I beat my arms across my body to drive out the cold, but I had to stop as our fragile craft started to heave up and down in unison. In frustration I flung off my sodden flying helmet and watched it arcing across the sea, trailing the intercom cord like a kite doomed to destruction.

The wireless operator found a flare and French-Mullen gave him permission to set it off. It rose with a swish high above us. It never occurred to us that we were making our position known to the enemy. All we wanted was to get to dry land – any dry land.

About two hours later, I saw luminous sprays breaking the horizon. They grew larger, and presently I saw the bow washes of two small boats heading towards us. Soon they came alongside and we were pulled aboard: the N.C.O.s in one boat and the officers in the other. Before I parted from French-Mullen, he pressed something into my hand. A quick glance revealed a piece of hacksaw blade. A fleeting image of a dungeon and iron bars flashed into my mind.

'This is the boat I machine-gunned!' exclaimed the rear gunner loudly as he clambered on to the deck.

'I hope for our sakes it isn't,' I hissed.

'They can't understand English,' he retorted defiantly.

'Don't bank on it. For Christ's sake pipe down,' I said.

The three of us went below into a cramped, dimly lit cabin where a young man and a lad of about twelve years offered us black coffee and hunks of rye bread. I had no stomach for either and indicated my desire to go up on deck. There were no objections.

I wandered about, beating my arms, trying to dry off in the breeze and in the rays of the rising sun, but unable to dismiss the chill of wet underwear clinging to my bare skin.

The motor-driven boat was about 30 feet in length with a small bridge and wheelhouse in which a giant of a man stood at the helm. I saw no signs of fish, but I discovered our dinghy lashed to the mast; inside there was a large jack-knife and a loaded Verey pistol. I picked the pistol up and turned with it in my hand to face the bridge. The helmsman reacted immediately, shouting, 'Nein!

Nein …!' He was obviously frightened and unaware that, as a weapon, the Verey pistol was next to useless. An attempt to take over the boat by bluff crossed my mind, but I dismissed the idea instantly, having no stomach for terrorising our rescuers, one of whom was a mere lad – probably the skipper's son. I flung the pistol back, waved at the agitated helmsman and settled myself down in the bows on a coil of rope.

A thin mist was now swirling over the surface of the sea, blotting out any hope of seeing our destination. Suddenly, unfamiliar black objects were bobbing about in the swell on the port side. The young man came up on deck carrying a long pole. He stepped across me and stood in the bows to push the horned objects out of our path. We were passing through a minefield! I prayed that he was skilled at his work.

Soon the mist lifted and an island of red rock loomed into sight. We anchored in a small harbour and followed our rescuers up stone steps on to the jetty, to be greeted by a hostile crowd of civilians who spat at us and shook fists in our faces. Fortunately, we were met by three soldiers who escorted us through narrow streets to a tunnel entrance at the foot of a steep cliff.

We soon found ourselves in a subterranean fortress with rooms hewn out of the solid rock. (Rather like something out of a James Bond film.) We were then locked in separate cells.

After a brief interrogation, I was given a beaker of ersatz coffee, followed by a change of underwear. In the early afternoon, we were escorted back to harbour, where we embarked on a pleasure boat for Wilhelmshaven, accompanied by armed guards and dozens of young blonde-headed Germans participating in a 'Kraft durch Freude' (Strength Through Joy) excursion. We sat below deck listening to the singing of patriotic songs from above and getting an occasional inquisitive glance from curious girls who had ventured to the top of the companionway.

Through a porthole, I could see the island fortress receding into the distance. 'Heliogoland?' I said to one of the guards.

'Ja,' he replied.

Ffrench-Mullen wandered over to where I was seated and we exchanged thoughts. 'How do you think we will be treated, sir?' I said.

'I don't know, Donaldson,' he replied, 'but things haven't been too bad so far.'

I thought about the kindness of the fishermen. They didn't seem a bad lot – not a bit like the stories I'd heard. I remembered the German boy who had looked at me with such pity in his eyes. I'd given him all my loose coins – it was a rather crude way of showing my appreciation for being pulled out of the North Sea. I hope he didn't look upon it as a kind of gratuity. I wanted it simply to be a token that, in later years, would remind him of the day he helped to save the lives of British airmen who had come to bomb his homeland.

The naval authorities at Wilhelmshaven took scant interest in us and we were soon bustled on a train bound for Frankfurt, accompanied by two guards and an Alsatian dog which, having devoured my unwanted ration of sausage, became very friendly and spent most of the journey with his head on my knees.

The handler didn't seem to mind this display of fraternisation with the enemy. However, he made it clear that giving scarce food to a well-fed dog was foolish and that I would see the wisdom of his words when I was an inmate of a prisoner-of-war camp.

The other guard, a small man with sad eyes, remained silent throughout most of the journey and only became agitated when some civilians tried to enter our compartment. The Nazi salutes and Heil Hitlers did nothing to stop the loud and meaningless abuse which he directed at the would-be intruders. Only when the door had been firmly shut in their faces did he return to his seat and his former state of melancholy.

The landscape unfolding through the carriage window seemed

almost like the one I used to watch en route from York to King's Cross when I went home on leave. There were the grimy industrial towns – places I had only known as names on a target map. I looked for signs of bomb damage but saw little. There were busy market towns and villages with well-kept gardens and orchards heavy with fruit. There were fields and woodlands, and occasionally there were glimpses of children at play and horses pulling farm carts.

'Deutsche Fülle,' (German wealth) said the dog handler, pointing to a forest of fir trees.

Then suddenly the journey was over and we were being escorted across a busy main line station towards the exit. We were walking in single file, with sad-eyes leading and the dog handler taking up the rear, when a strange thing happened which I have never been able to explain to my satisfaction. As we forced our way through the milling crowd – doubtless looking rather dejected – a man stepped across my path, almost causing me to trip up. As he brushed past, he said softly, 'Cheer up, matey, you'll be all right.'

I turned quickly but he had vanished in the crowd.

A British agent? If he was, he was taking a quite unnecessary risk. Whoever he was, I would like to record my appreciation of this act of human good-heartedness. It boosted my morale and I walked to the waiting army truck with my head held a little higher.

The transit camp near Frankfurt had been established to interrogate aircrew before dispersing them to other camps throughout Germany. Here, the five of us were imprisoned in separate cells and only met briefly during visits to the washroom and lavatories.

My cell light was never turned off, and whenever I slumped exhausted into a deep sleep, I would be rudely awakened for another bout of questioning.

'Your mother will be very worried about you when she hears

you are missing. The shock could give her a heart attack ... If you fill in this Red Cross form here ... yes, you must put down the number of your squadron and where it is based and, of course, the name of your commanding officer ... then we can get the news of your capture immediately to England. ... What kind of aircraft did you say you were flying?'

'I can only give you my name, rank and number.'

'Well now, you're not being very co-operative, are you? Not like the rest of your crew. They have already told me where you were based. Dishforth, wasn't it? And the clock in Ripon market place, is it still running ten minutes slow?'

And so the interrogations proceeded, sometimes with a packet of Players pushed in my direction, sometimes with hints of the consequences which would overtake me if I remained stubborn.

The questioners were usually smart, well-spoken young Luftwaffe officers. They must have found this haggard youth difficult to assess, for I was too tired to respond, and their smooth voices soon faded into a monotonous, disembodied drone on the fringes of my consciousness.

Then it was all over and I joined the rest of the crew behind the barbed wire in the main camp.

'What kept you so long?' asked Ffrench-Mullen.

'I've been telling them my life story, sir.'

'Some bugger's been telling them too much. They knew we came from Dishforth and that Staton was our C.O.,' said the rear gunner, eyeing me suspiciously.

'Well, it's not me,' I said indignantly.

But perhaps it was me. Perhaps I'd been talking in my sleep. Perhaps I'd become so confused that my waking and sleeping moments had merged to entrap me in a kind of trance ...

'It doesn't matter, anyway,' said the skipper. 'They probably already know more about Bomber Command than we do.'

After a few days in Frankfurt, we entrained for a prison camp situated at Barth near Stralsund on the Baltic coast.

So began for me what was to be a long period of captivity, stretching over almost five years, encompassing camps in Poland, central Germany, Lithuania and other far-flung outposts of the Third Reich.

When Red Cross food parcels came through, life was bearable, but when we depended entirely on rations doled out by our captors, we eked out an existence on the borders of starvation. At such times, fresh-faced youngsters became hollow-cheeked old men, preserving their wilting energies by staying prone in their wooden bunks for weeks at a time.

Even worse than this was the lack of fresh physical and mental stimuli, bringing about a state of dull indifference to everything except the size of one's bread ration or the lice sucking one's blood in the depths of the night. Of course, with as many as a hundred men sharing a communal existence in a barrack hut, one had little peace to indulge in self-pity or find escape in the pages of a well-thumbed book. There was no privacy in prison camps.

The officers fared a little better than the N.C.O.s, for they had more spacious accommodation, but the basic food ration was the same for everybody. In one respect, however, the N.C.O.s were better off – they could get beyond the barbed wire by volunteering for work. This earned a bigger bread ration and the contempt of one's fellow prisoners for aiding the enemy war effort. Some were prepared to accept the ostracism in order to experience a transitory freedom – however false – on the country road leading to the local market town where prisoners were employed.

Others, like myself, saw working parties as providing opportunities to breach the first obstacles obstructing would-be escapers: the warning wire with its comical sign which read, 'DO NOT APPROACH THIS WIRE OR IT WILL BE SHOT'; the high double barbed-wire fence overlooked by numerous postern towers equipped with machine-guns; the searchlights and arc lights which illuminated every section of the perimeter; and the armed guards who patrolled night and day. Bypass this system and you could be half-way home by Christmas – at least, that was what I thought in the summer of 1941, after a year in captivity.

Secrecy was imperative, so Ali Stamford and I walked endlessly round the compound, discussing our plans. At that time it was thought that the Germans had planted a spy, disguised as a prisoner, to gather information; so we weren't taking any risks.

Ali was a small, tough Eurasian who seemed able to endure privations with a calm, cheerful stoicism which I greatly admired. He displayed a resourcefulness and a planning ability which enabled us to join a working party employed in the local gasworks. He had another talent which was to prove useful in furthering our escape: he could discipline himself to save food from his meagre rations without impairing the fitness of his slim, muscular body. He encouraged me to do likewise but I found the pangs of hunger hard to endure.

Ali and I were housed in different billets, so I had no first-hand knowledge of how his room-mates reacted to his decision to work for the enemy. He never broached the subject and neither did I inform him about the sudden nose-dive in my popularity, which reached rock bottom on the evening before our intended escape.

With a view to boosting my hidden store of chocolate, I had done some trading with a friendly guard whom I had been cultivating for some time.

'Anyone who deals with those bastards should have their blocks knocked off.' The comment was made for my benefit by George Grimson (who later became the most wanted escaper in Germany).

'If you think you could do it, Grimson, why don't you come

and try?' My challenge was spoken with face-saving bravado but inwardly I felt scared, for Grimson was a muscular fellow who would probably flatten me with one blow.

'Right, Donaldson, outside in the corridor then – you'll only return to this room unconscious over my shoulder.'

We both went into the corridor, followed by a crowd of onlookers, keen to make the most of this unexpected diversion.

I guessed right, Grimson did flatten me with his first punch. Then, grasping my lapels, he butted me with his head and I fell backwards on a hard, unyielding floor. In vain, I struggled to rise but he was soon sitting astride me with a fist raised to strike. I threw my head to one side and the blow landed harmlessly on the floor. Before he could repeat the attack I heaved myself off the floor and landed a punch to his face. Blood oozed from his mouth. But my guardian angel must have been on duty that night for I heard an air-raid siren wailing above the cheers and then suddenly the whole gathering was enveloped in darkness.

We were both taken by surprise. I could hear heavy breathing near the shuttered windows and struck out again, feeling a stab of pain as my knuckle hit something sharp. I could hear the spectators drifting away and then someone shouted, 'Pack it in, you silly buggers!'

'I'll see you behind the cookhouse before morning appell. We'll finish it then,' gasped a voice that didn't sound much like Grimson's.

The lights never came on again that night and I lay in the dark trying to compose myself, but no sooner had I dispelled the images of the fight than new, more terrorising ones came to take their place. Tomorrow was the day – the day I would live or die. It was too late to back out now, for the fear of cowardice was stronger than the fear of death. If only I could discuss things with Ali. Go over our plans again. I began wondering how he was bearing up. Was he shivering beneath blankets on this warm summer's night – shivering with fear? Not Ali, his self-discipline would be keeping his fear firmly under control. In all probability he would be in a deep sleep, preparing his mind and body for the dangers which would come with the dawn when the guards unlocked the shutters.

I rose early and caught a glimpse of Grimson making for the wash house. He had a bruised cheek and one of his front teeth looked broken. I felt ashamed of what I'd done. We were supposed to be fighting the Germans – not each other. I made up my mind to shake his hand before I left to join Ali and the other members of the working party at the main gate.

I was sitting on my bunk drinking a mug of mint tea when he returned. He walked up to me, grinning, with his hand extended.

'Going on holiday?' he said, eyeing a bulging haversack which I was attempting to conceal inside a greatcoat slung over my arm.

I winked at him and walked out into the bright sunlight with a renewed sense of confidence, leaving behind – hopefully for ever – the familiar smell of stale urine emanating from the block lavatories.

There were eight of us in the working party, which was searched at the vorlager gate. I stood anxiously with my arms outstretched, trying to hold the coat without noticeable effort, feeling my side and breast pockets patted in the usual slipshod fashion; yet expecting any moment to hear a triumphant shout as the contents of my haversack scattered on the ground.

'Alles in ordnung!' (Everything in order.)

I breathed again as the two armed guards shepherded us into some kind of order before escorting us along the footpath, leading to the small town just visible through the trees. Ali walked alongside in silence, unaware of my thumping heart and my left arm trembling with its concealed weight.

'So far, so good,' I whispered.

He nodded and then it came on to rain. It was so unexpected

because we had left the camp in bright sunshine ten minutes previously. The shower was heavy and one of the guards shouted at me to put my coat on. I shrugged as if it were a matter of little consequence and walked on, damp and unrepentant, like a defiant village idiot.

Ali was getting equally wet but he looked less ridiculous for he was not carrying a coat – his haversack, containing items of civilian clothing for both of us, had already been secreted in a toilet at our place of work. My haversack contained the food, maps and a compass.

The rain stopped as quickly as it had started, and by the time we had reached the gasworks our clothes were beginning to steam in the warmth of the sun.

The plan was simple. We both worked in the gasworks yard, shovelling coke into a crushing machine. The other six prisoners were employed in the same area, digging trenches and carrying out general labouring work. One of them had agreed to aid our escape.

The two guards stood or walked aimlessly about, often chatting together to dispel the boredom of their duty. Sometimes they stood alone, having a quiet smoke or engaging a prisoner in conversation. (Once a fatherly individual, who thought I was not using my shovel to the best advantage, told me to hold his rifle whilst he gave me a demonstration!)

Prisoners requiring to use the lavatory asked permission from the nearest guard: it was rarely refused. The lavatory block had been built against the tall boundary wall and was also used by the German workers manning the furnaces. An examination of the interior of this building made over a period of several weeks had revealed a door and a window overlooking a narrow alley which led down to the harbour. The door was kept locked but the window pivoted in a horizontal plane, providing sufficient space through which a determined person of small stature might squeeze.

Ali and I made sure that we were well separated so that we could seek permission from different guards. Ali asked first and was given the usual wave of consent. I waited a minute and approached the other guard, who told me to wait as there was already a prisoner in there. I bent down slightly and brought my knees together whilst assuming an expression of intense discomfort, as if I were about to empty the contents of my bowels at his feet. He hesitated and then pointed to the door through which Ali had disappeared.

I put my shovel down, picked up my coat and walked quickly across the yard.

As soon as I got through the door, I sensed something was wrong. I was greeted by grunts and groans and the sounds of creaking timbers, and the spectacle of Ali struggling to get through the top section of the window, his legs thrashing the air behind him.

'For Christ's sake, either get through or get out of it!' I shouted in panic. As Ali had his head hanging over the outside passage, it became obvious that he could neither hear nor see me. Pushing his backside seemed only to jam him more firmly into the aperture.

I grabbed the door handle in an attempt to lever myself up on to the windowsill. Slowly the door gave and freedom was staring me in the face. I pulled Ali backwards by his boots and saw him shoot into the lavatory like a cork from a bottle. Still holding his haversack, he scrambled after me, then he went calmly back and shut the door.

Before reaching the end of the alley, we threw off our R.A.F. tunics and put on our homemade civilian jackets and peaked caps. We hoped to pass ourselves off as Polish workers by displaying the mandatory 'P' on our lapels, but we didn't fool the Polish workers near the harbour, who gazed at us in stunned amazement, giving us the thumbs-up sign as we headed east across the market. We passed the police station and walked briskly out of town, looking for a minor road to take us up the coast to Stralsund, where we hoped to get a boat to Sweden.

Once we'd left the town behind, the road straightened out, cutting across a sunlit patchwork of fields to disappear between some distant buildings. There was an uncanny quietness – no traffic, no pedestrians, just the drone of a distant plane crossing our line of vision.

'What do you think those buildings are?'

Ali narrowed his eyes, deepening the lines that scored his gaunt, sunburnt face. 'They're hangars,' he replied.

We were heading directly for an airfield, and continued to do so as if mesmerised by the planes which we could now see dispersed behind a high wire fence.

Fleeting, irrational thoughts stirred my imagination, to be quickly rejected. Neither of us could fly. Even if we could hijack one of … The thoughts kept returning … 'Two of our airmen escaped from a prisoner-of-war camp today and crash-landed a stolen enemy plane in a field near … they have both been recommended for …'

'We'll take that lane,' said Ali, bringing me back to reality. He was pointing to a track which rose gradually from the airfield between fields of ripe corn.

We soon reached the top of the incline, to find an embankment which had been concealed from the road.

'That'll be the railway!' I exclaimed, running the last few yards to the top of the slope.

'Our way,' said Ali, pointing to the single track of polished rails glistening in the sun.

I sat down and took a swig from my water bottle, conscious of the sweat beneath my coarse, ill-fitting jacket.

'Are you suggesting that we should walk along there in broad daylight?'

'Have you got a better idea, Donaldson?'

Ali always used my surname when he was cross with me.

Now we argued and I gave vent to my tension with a display of bad-tempered impatience.

'Now look, Ali, what you are suggesting is absolute suicide. We must wait until nightfall before going any further. You saw the way the Poles looked at us in the harbour – we didn't fool them and we are not likely to fool the Germans either.'

Ali shrugged his shoulders and let me have my way. We followed the embankment for a short distance before skirting a harvest field dotted with sheaves of wheat.

'That's what we're looking for,' I said.

'Is it?' commented Ali without a trace of conviction.

'Come on, help me to make a hideout with these sheaves. Nobody will find us here.'

It was now midday and the sun beat down on us from a cloudless blue sky. We were soon sweltering in our makeshift tents of straw – so much so that we rolled up our trousers and stuck our legs outside in an attempt to cool off. Matters came to a head when we discovered that low-flying aircraft approaching the airfield were passing directly over our position.

'It's no good, we'll have to move,' I said.

'Come on, Peter, let's get going. You're probably right about the railway – the bridges are likely to be guarded. Let's continue along the lane – it runs roughly in the direction we want to go.'

We crossed the railway and picked up the track on the other side. We walked slowly, drinking in the freedom – four hours of it – scenting the wild flowers mixed with the musty smell of dried grass and feeling a gentle breeze in our faces. Even if we were recaptured now, it would have been worth it just for these few hours without a barbed-wire fence or a guard in sight.

As we walked, we discussed our undignified escape from the lavatory block. 'It is amazing one of the guards didn't come to find out what we were up to – particularly after all the time spent getting you unjammed,' I said.

'Not so amazing as you think. I'd briefed Tiny Bushell about our intentions and he had agreed to walk towards the main gate if either of the guards became suspicious quickly. I know Tiny well – he wouldn't let us down.'

'Why didn't you tell me that before?' I asked.

'Secrecy, my friend, secrecy,' replied Ali, tapping his nose.

I was about to suggest that one could take secrecy too far when a large vehicle came bumping into sight round a curve in the lane. We both stepped hastily to one side and then stood rooted to the spot as a truck-load of soldiers careered past. They were singing and I caught the words 'Gegen England'. We waved at them and they waved back.

The incident seemed to give us confidence. Had we not just fooled a unit of the Wehrmacht? Perhaps our disguises were more convincing than we had thought. The lane now widened into a road, along which we continued to walk with renewed confidence. After several miles we came to the outskirts of a village, where a group of children were playing in front of a house. They stood in silence as we walked by, eyeing us with undisguised curiosity. We pressed on with a growing sense of unease.

In the distance I saw a man about to mount a bicycle: his hands were on the handlebars and his right leg poised over the saddle when he looked up and saw us.

'What shall we do, Ali? Make a run for it?'

'We'll bluff it out,' he replied.

The man was now standing with his hands on his hips, waiting for us, and as we came nearer we saw he was a policeman. There was no turning back now.

For a moment I thought he was going to ignore us but he stepped out to block our way. 'Wo gehen sie?' he shouted.

'Stralsund,' I answered.

He was a corpulent man and his podgy hands fumbled with the holster on the belt under his ample belly. 'Halt!' he shouted.

I was now looking down the barrel of a revolver levelled at a point about mid-way between my eyebrows. I didn't wait for further orders but put both hands above my head. Ali, slightly behind me, followed my example.

We were marched into a nearby house which turned out to be his home-cum-village police station. Once in his office, he whipped off my cap and said, 'Ah, blond!' He then sat behind a desk, placing his gun in front of him whilst on the wall behind Adolf Hitler looked down with approval. Keeping his eyes on us, he picked up the phone. After two 'Heil Hitlers' and a Nazi salute he engaged in conversation with somebody who obviously had our descriptions. With my limited knowledge of the German language, I was able to learn that the commandant was sending transport to pick us up.

Once the phone call had ended, the policeman seemed more relaxed. He returned the gun to its holster and called for his wife and teenage daughter, whom he obviously wanted to impress. Had he not arrested two English airmen single-handed?

The young girl spoke good English and she looked at us with sadness in her eyes. Knowing our food supplies would soon be confiscated, I offered her some chocolate. She glanced at her mother and then refused, saying it was forbidden to accept gifts from prisoners of war.

Her mother was one of those people who get satisfaction from hitting their opponents when they're down.

'Our submarines have sunk 700,000 tons of your shipping,' she crowed.

'Propaganda,' I countered.

'Soon our Führer will invade England and the war will be over.'

'Tell your mother,' I said, 'Winston Churchill has got a different plan.' Inwardly, however, I felt that the prophecy of this policeman's wife might possibly be fulfilled.

Despite the antagonism I was displaying towards his wife, the policeman remained affable and immensely pleased with himself. Using his daughter as an interpreter, he explained how foolish we were to be heading for Stralsund, which was a port strictly forbidden to all Polish workers. It appeared that we would have been arrested even if we had been bone fide Poles.

Ali looked thoroughly dejected and gave vent to his feelings from time to time with bouts of swearing. My own disappointment was tempered with a sense of satisfaction that we had at least won a few hours of freedom and that, although our efforts were doomed to failure – in the light of what the policeman had told us – we had nevertheless proved that the German system of security was not infallible.

In due course a Luftwaffe car arrived and we were driven back to camp, wedged on the rear seat between two bulky guards. I spent most of the journey devouring half a pound of chocolate, and by the time the escort reached the vorlager, I felt sick.

The commandant rose from behind a polished desk, adjusted the Iron Cross ribbon on his immaculate Luftwaffe uniform and passed a sinewy hand through his close-cropped hair. He was tall and sported duelling scars on both cheeks. The greeting was that of a benevolent headmaster. 'You are very naughty boys. Are you not happy here? Why you want to escape?'

I explained it was our duty to escape.

He nodded and went on to describe his own experiences as a prisoner of war in England during the 1914-18 war. 'I was well treated. Your treatment here is good, yes?'

Ali made a grimace and the questioner looked hurt.

Relieved that we were not facing an arrogant Nazi, I tried to keep the interview friendly. 'Our treatment is not bad,' I said, 'but the food is poor and we are always hungry when there are no Red Cross parcels.'

'You get the same food as the men who guard you, but for the next two weeks you will live only on bread and water in solitary confinement.'

Other questions followed, aimed at discovering how we were able to take food and clothing through the security check at the main gate. The commandant frowned and summoned an orderly. It seemed that the unfortunate guard responsible for searching us would have some answering to do himself.

'I will let you return to your comrades now, gentlemen. Tomorrow you will start your punishment in the cooler.'

The reception waiting for us in the compound took us both by surprise. We were carried shoulder-high into our respective huts to be back-patted and plied with questions. There was a whip-round for items of food and I was soon sitting before a slap-up meal, glowing in the unaccustomed attention and flattery.

I felt very sorry for George Grimson. He had seen me doing deals with German guards with whom I exchanged tobacco for various items of food. He was a pipe-smoker and wrongly assumed I was profiteering at the expense of my fellow prisoners. He obviously felt that he could no longer share a billet with the first N.C.O. to escape from Stalag Luft I. He gathered up his meagre belongings and found refuge in another billet occupied by disabled prisoners. He spent the next two years studying German and became the most proficient speaker in the camp.

(I didn't see George again until I was reunited with him and my former colleagues in Stalag Luft III, following the completion of my 'holiday' in a punishment camp. We embraced each other. A few days later, I watched him climb over a double barbed-wire fence, disguised as a German security guard. He escaped without being challenged. During the following eight to nine months he set up an escape route from Danzig to Sweden. He once returned to the camp disguised as a plumber to give vital information to the escape committee. He was finally caught by the Gestapo, tortured and shot. A recommendation for a V.C. was turned down.)

They came for me early one morning and I was marched to the

cooler to begin my sentence in a cell little bigger than a domestic lavatory. It was furnished with a bucket and a low wooden platform on which were folded two blankets and a thin straw palliasse. The heavy metal door had a glass spy hole through which I could see, from time to time, an eye peering at me from the corridor. Opposite the door, there was a small barred window, beyond my reach, displaying a small rectangle of ever-changing sky.

I marked each day off by making scratches on the whitewashed walls with a fork I had secreted under a blanket. The diet of bread and water was insufficient in quantity and nourishment. I suspected that the French orderlies who served me with this fare were stealing a good portion of it for themselves. I met Ali in the washroom one day, and he had arrived at a similar conclusion.

I remember the morning well: it was June 22nd 1941. I had five more days of solitary to serve. A guard entered my cell with a jug of water. He spoke a smattering of English. 'German forces have advanced into Russia. It is very bad. Now we can no longer win the war. Soon we shall have to fight on two fronts.' He was almost in tears.

This unexpected news, together with the guard's prophecy, lifted my depression and sent my spirits soaring. Now I could see that an Allied victory was possible.

At exactly two weeks to the minute after the start of my confinement, I thumped with both fists on the door of the cell to gain the attention of the guards. One came running down the corridor and unlocked the door to confront me. Why was I making such a rumpus? Was I sick in the head? I explained that the commandant had given me two weeks and my release was already one minute overdue.

The guard left to make inquiries, and twenty minutes later I was walking weakly back to the compound, accompanied by the other 'naughty boy'.

In the days ahead, I didn't see much of Ali. I certainly har-

Stalag Luft III

boured no ill feeling towards him but I got the impression that he blamed me for our recapture – for not agreeing to his suggestion of walking along the railway track instead of the road. However, neither of us had much time to ponder what might have been, for one morning early in July the German officer in charge of the morning appell had some grave news. After the count, he called out the numbers of twelve prisoners, including mine and Ali's. We were ordered to take one step forward whilst the rest of the prisoners were dismissed and locked in their huts. The officer beckoned us to him. 'Gentlemen,' he said, 'I have some very bad news for you. By order of the High Command you are all being sent immediately to a punishment camp. It is not good for you and I am very sorry. Please get your kit together and assemble at the main gate in five minutes.'

We were a mixed bunch. Apart from Ali and me, there was 'Tiny' Bushell, ex-all-in wrestler, who had helped us to escape. There was Victor Savage, better known as 'the Monk', who had been caught red-handed making civilian clothes. There were others who had got their names on the blacklist for a variety of reasons, ranging from derogatory remarks about our captors written in letters home, to physical violence directed at a guard by a sergeant pilot who endured six months' solitary confinement for this lapse in self-control.

We were escorted from the compound by a squad of guards and locked in an empty hut – at least, so it seemed until close examination revealed several microphones hidden behind wooden panels. These were soon ripped out.

Then 'Tiny' started jumping on the floor.

'This floor is loose,' he said, thumping up and down with his eighteen stones as if he were back in the ring again. Within a few minutes the whole floor had taken on a crazy angle. A great commotion started outside and the door burst open to the sound of our cheers, which became somewhat muted when the fixed bayonets came into sight.

Now we were prodded outside and lined up to be harangued by an elderly, somewhat wizened officer who screamed at us in a high pitched voice: 'Anyone escape, immediate shooting!' We all laughed, which brought him to the verge of hysteria.

There followed a long, uncomfortable train journey to Lamdsdorf on the borders of Czechoslovakia. We were accompanied by the overwrought officer, now nicknamed 'Weasel', and six guards who had obviously been briefed to treat us all like hardened criminals.

In the late afternoon of the following day, we arrived at a small station where we were assembled on the platform to be subjected to another chorus of 'immediate shootings'. We were too hungry and dejected to react with the high spirits we had shown at the start of the journey.

My limbs soon lost their stiffness as I marched along a country road, carrying all my treasured possessions in a homemade haversack. I saw a large cemetery with row upon row of white wooden crosses stretching almost to the horizon. Feeling apprehensive, I asked the nearest guard what it all meant.

'Russian prisoners who died of typhus in the 1918 war,' he replied. His answer did little to dispel my fears.

Soon we approached the entrance to a large camp with the now familiar wooden towers and high barbed-wire fences, behind which stood groups of men clothed in shabby khaki battledress. Their shaven heads and pale, gaunt faces contrasted strongly with the cheerful cockney voices which commanded us to throw our watches and other valuables over the wire before we were searched.

'I'd rather trust the Jerries than that lot,' said Todd Hawkins, whose inclusion on the blacklist was probably due to our friendship – we had both been shot down on the same day.

The search was thorough. They were not interested in my watch, but they took a fur-lined leather jacket which my mother had managed to get to me through the British Red Cross Society.

'That's my personal property,' I complained. 'According to the Geneva Convention, you have no legal right to confiscate it.'

The Feldwebel was not impressed. 'That is an Air Force flying jacket and we have a right to take it. However, we will give you a receipt.'

I was forced to hand it over. Had I known that the worst winter for seventy years was about to ravage eastern Europe, I would have felt even more enraged by this act of inhumanity.

Soon we were led to a small compound within a huge complex of compounds where most of the 30,000 soldiers captured at Dunkirk were billeted.

Thus began two years of hunger and deprivation. There were no Red Cross food parcels and little fuel to heat the bare concrete buildings in which we were housed. Our diet consisted of black bread, swede and thin soup. To add to our discomfort we soon became infested with lice, which we were told could be carriers of the dreaded typhus germ.

The worst time was during the winter of 1941–42 when the temperature dropped to depths I had never experienced before. Frostbite and malnutrition were commonplace – the struggle to survive seemed to direct every thought and every action. The fair distribution of a loaf shared between eight prisoners assumed a significance which in hindsight I can remember and understand. Stripped of the veneer of civilisation, educated *Homo sapiens* can find himself controlled by a primitive instinct which will have no truck with charity and unselfishness. As hunger gnaws at your guts, you may not steal from your best friend, but you'll certainly do so from your enemies. On more than one occasion, I volunteered to help unload a Wehrmacht bread lorry with the specific aim of supplementing my rations.

There were two dates in the winter of 1941 which remained with me. October 29th, my twenty-first birthday – I was lying on my bunk, huddled in blankets, trying to keep warm, when a hand came from nowhere holding a small address book. 'Happy Birthday, Peter!' said Todd, his bearded face grinning from behind a frost-encrusted balaclava helmet.

Later that same day, the lights had died earlier than usual and there was barely time to don my own woollen nightcap and creep further under my ersatz blankets before the window shutters were slammed, plunging the freezing barrack hut into darkness.

I occupied a top bunk above a less fortunate, lanky Australian sergeant pilot whose closer proximity to the floor exposed him to attack from rats, which I could now hear crunching their way in beneath the floorboards. Their targets for tonight were the protruding toes of careless prisoners.

Then there were other noises denying me escape to dreams of clean, white, lice-free sheets and mountains of beef and Yorkshire puddings. I could just hear the drone of high-flying aircraft. Others heard it too, and someone shouted, 'Give it to the buggers!'

I listened for the thud of exploding bombs but no more sounds were heard – even the rats seemed to have gone quiet. Then miraculously a new sound filled the black void, a sound long forgotten that stirred memories of other days and nights when men were free and well fed. Frank Hunt was a violinist of great talent and sensitivity who had managed to cling to his treasured instrument through all the trials of his captivity. Now, dressed in a shabby trench coat, he strolled between the rows of double bunks warming our hearts with old favourites. Thank you, Frank. I would have given you my soup ration for an encore! And thank you, Royal Air Force, for giving me fresh hope on my twenty-first birthday.

The other date was Christmas Eve. I was dreaming of turkey, plum pudding and mince pies when I heard a rifle shot. The noise in the barrack wound down like a spent gramophone record. I squinted through a hole in a shutter at the moonlit snow in the compound. At first I could see nothing but the searchlights beaming on a section of fence directly in line with my spy hole. When my eye became accustomed to the brightness, I saw a man standing beyond the warning wire with both hands above his head. A guard ran into my line of sight. He was shouting. Then he stopped, raised his gun and fired. The figure in front of him slumped to the ground, and slowly the snow around the fallen body became tinged with red. That was Sergeant Reid, who died on Christmas Eve.

The days of chivalry, of mutual respect between captors and captives, were passing. Now all Germans were bastards. There was no excuse for shooting an unarmed prisoner in cold blood – not even if you were a trigger-happy soldaten brutalised by the merciless campaign on the Eastern Front. Others were to die that winter – most of them were Russians guilty of the offence of trying to steal an extra bowl of soup.

I said to a German officer (christened 'Bullock's Piss' for describing a rank of prisoners in these terms), 'Why do you treat the Russians like animals?'

'Because they are like animals,' he replied.

As the cruel weather continued throughout early spring, the Russian compound became little more than a slaughtering ground. Hundreds of starving, gaunt-faced, ragged men marched round a barbed-wire enclosure, singing national songs until one by one they dropped, exhausted, to die in the snow. For those who survived, their only protection from the fearful conditions was an open trench; their only food was a small ration of watery soup. It was a harrowing ordeal to watch and hear the sad, heroic voices lifted in song, seeming to raise the human spirit above the wretchedness of war.

So the weeks of my imprisonment passed but slowly, highlighted by an occasional letter or parcel from home or by an important news item heard on our secret radio – which could be dismantled and distributed round a barrack block in less than a minute prior to an imminent search.

Another kind of break in the monotony was a transfer to a different prison camp. The first was to Königsberg on the borders of Lithuania, where my friends and I stayed for a year until we were evacuated in haste by cattle truck with the faint rumble of Russian guns to cheer us on our way.

It was always difficult to know what to take and what to leave on these occasions – long-serving prisoners like myself tended to collect more than we could carry. I had acquired a set of leather-bound poetry books – Keats, Shelley, Longfellow etc. Concerned as I always was with survival, I decided to leave them behind in favour of additional warm clothing. I offered them to a German interpreter who had been particularly friendly and co-operative in helping to get me some art materials.

'I cannot accept these,' he said, 'although I would like to own them very much. You see, soon I shall be posted to an anti-aircraft unit in France. I could not fire at your comrades knowing that I had accepted this gift from you.'

Some of the prisoners were less pragmatic than I was, and preferred to go without food and clothing rather than leave some treasured object. One such was a gifted violinist. Unfortunately, his plans for his treasured instrument went tragically wrong. A few minutes before we were due to depart, an over-enthusiastic rear gunner went round his billet systematically destroying anything which could be of use to the Germans. He put his foot through the unattended violin whilst the owner was paying a final visit to the toilet.

After Königsberg, I spent a few months at a camp near Thorn in Poland. It was here that the escape committee decided it was time I made another attempt. In spite of searches by the camp authorities and later by a large detachment of Gestapo, the committee had been able to reach Thorn with most of their equipment intact. This included a camera, several complete German uniforms, printing materials, travel warrants, identity cards and even permits to travel signed by the local chief of police – all forged, of course. In addition, they had acquired a pair of wire cutters, several compasses, an assortment of maps and a useful sum of German marks. Most, if not all, of these items had been obtained by bribery or blackmail. The technique was to tempt guards to bring in forbidden goods with offers of coffee or cigarettes, saved from rare food parcels. Initially, approaches would be made to the carefully chosen victim for such trivial things as razor blades, cotton and thread, but once the unsuspecting German had been persuaded to widen his shopping list to include petrol, photographic paper, army badges etc., he was firmly enmeshed in the committee's web of intrigue. If he struggled, he would be reminded that the penalty for trading with prisoners was an immediate posting to the Eastern Front – in other words, a death sentence.

With these methods it soon became possible to borrow identity cards, travel warrants and other passes which were then copied by a small group of forgers who had no shortage of time to develop their skills. The Gestapo eventually got near the fringes of this organisation. A German camp photographer committed suicide, and several members of the escape committee were escorted from the camp, never to be seen again. My own involvement in these procurement operations was brief, amusing and somewhat hazardous. The committee asked me to obtain a large bottle of petrol – at least a litre was required. One never sought to find out to what purpose a substance would be put, so I agreed to do my best without any questions.

I selected a tall, cheerful guard from a solemn-faced contingent recently returned from the Eastern Front. It was a cold, frosty day – not one for hanging about after appell. I approached him directly as he was about to march out of the compound.

'Could you get me some petrol? I have some spare English cigarettes,' I said, walking alongside, trying to keep in step with his long strides. Speaking from the corner of his mouth, he replied, 'Jawohl, Morgen.'

My first impression had been correct. He seemed cast in that military mould that looked upon war as an unpleasant activity which should, as far as possible, be turned to one's personal advantage. The wink he gave me as he turned to disappear through the compound gate was a final confirmation that I had chosen wisely.

The following morning I kept a lookout for my man. I spotted him easily, as he stood high above his fellow guards. He saw me too and, as soon as the count was over, he stepped openly towards me, put his hand inside his greatcoat and handed me a huge bottle without making any attempt to conceal his movements. I slipped a packet of cigarettes into his pocket and hurriedly pushed the bottle inside my battledress, expecting a harsh shout from the officer in charge – but none came.

The committee were delighted with my success and promised not to forget my name when sponsorships for potential escapers were being considered. This reaction brought me little comfort, as in recent months I had found it difficult to generate much enthusiasm for another attempt.

A week later, I was about to take leave of my sordid surroundings in the blessed imagery of sleep when I was startled by shouts and the sound of running feet. I looked towards the unshuttered window near my bunk. There were flickering reflections making patterns on the glass, and shadowy figures beyond trying to pull some kind of wheeled contraption. I was on my feet now, taking in the full spectacle. Just across the way, a wooden recreation hut was engulfed in flames and beneath my window the German equivalent of 'Dad's Army' was attempting to extinguish the inferno with equipment which might well have seen service in the First World War. No amount of bawling from the Unteroffizier in charge could increase the trickle of water spilling from the end of a solitary hosepipe. By the time a line of buckets had been organised, the fire had burnt itself out.

I was not surprised to learn, on the following morning, that four prisoners had escaped over the wire during the confusion. The petrol I had acquired had been put to good use.

At Thorn, I was called before the committee and told of their plans for me. They had reliable information that our stay there was only temporary and that all R.A.F. aircrew would be moved to a camp near Hanover in a few weeks' time.

The long-awaited news of the Allied invasion of Europe had already raised our hopes for an early end to the war. The prospect of travelling west, from where ultimate liberation would surely come, gave a further boost to our optimism. The members of the committee, however, did not hold this view, believing that the fighting in Europe might get bogged down for many months.

The plan at Thorn was to dig a large hole under one of the wooden huts in which we were housed. Sufficient space would be provided for two prisoners to conceal themselves whilst the camp was being evacuated. Once the coast was clear the escapees could cut through the unguarded fence and make their way to the local railway station, posing as Belgian munition workers en route to a factory in Austria not far from the Swiss border. A strong pair of wire cutters, civilian clothing, money, travel warrants and identity cards would be provided by the committee.

It seemed an attractive proposition and I began to feel quite excited. My companion, Sergeant Pilot Barnes, showed less enthusiasm, in spite of the fact that he was fluent in both German and French. His persistent prophecies of doom tended to unnerve me and I was glad when the final arrangements had been completed, when I was presented with my papers, including the identity card complete with photograph.

The day of departure dawned – a day of dank autumn smells with mist clinging to the trees beyond the wire. A final appell had been called, so Barnes and I quickly donned our civilian clothes, grabbed our suitcases and made for the hidey-hole, which we reached without detection.

After squatting in the damp earth for what seemed an age, we heard an urgent voice addressing us from above.

'For Christ's sake come out, you two. The Jerries have threatened to start shooting if there are any kriegies missing on the next appell. You've got about ten minutes to get yourselves organised.'

There was little time to spare, but we managed to join the final roll call, breathing heavily and carrying sufficient escape equipment to give any commandant a nervous breakdown. It was a risk we had to take if the escape committee were not to suffer further losses which, after the recent Gestapo raid, it could ill afford.

The journey westwards by cattle truck gave us plenty of time to ponder how we should deal with this and other problems. Progress was painfully slow, as Allied bombs had damaged several railway junctions: one such raid occurred whilst our train stood shunted in a siding to allow more important traffic through. We heard distant explosions and felt vibrations through the floor of the truck, and saw waving searchlight beams through the half-open door where our two guards sat hunched with their silent thoughts.

As the hours dragged by, I thought about the airmen overhead. To them this place was just a mark on a map – a target map. Unlike warriors of old, they hurled their spears of death even beyond the limits of their own imagination. At this moment, they would not be thinking of their victims or of the possibility that there might be British prisoners of war huddled in the darkness below. I knew about these things for I had, in what now seemed another life, been one of them.

Twice, ambulance trains, carrying wounded from the crumbling Eastern Front, passed slowly across the aperture like pictures on a cinema screen. Grim faces and bandaged limbs could be seen behind misted carriage windows. Once, a blond head rose from its stretcher and a hand was waved in salute. Although this gesture was probably meant for our guards, I felt a strong compulsion to acknowledge it. Were we not both victims of a senseless war? But I let the moment pass, fearing that my companions might not appreciate the response; particularly in view of the privations we were suffering as we jolted slowly westwards away from the advancing Russian armies.

Twenty prisoners were huddled at each end of our dark cattle truck, minus their shoes, belts and braces; separated from two guards by steel grilles which served to restrict movement and deny us access to the sliding doors.

I watched a pig-faced peasant in a crumpled green uniform sensually handling an English cigarette, passing it several times beneath his bulbous nose. I wanted to break out of my cage and push the brute out of the open door. I hated him for his bestial insensitivity.

When our train shuddered to a halt within a busy station, I started to hate all Germans, for we had stopped opposite a soup kitchen and I had to sit with parched mouth and cracked, swollen lips, watching the enemy spooning the rich brown liquid. Hate flooded into me, driving out the compassion I'd felt for the wounded soldier, and somehow giving me the strength and determination to survive.

Finally, after three days, we staggered out on to a platform at Hanover to be harangued by a pompous officer for our scruffy, unmilitary appearance. After much shouting, we were marched unceremoniously a few miles to Fallingsbostel and the prisoner-of-war camp from which I would ultimately escape.

Too weak to carry heavy loads, several marchers jettisoned some of their possessions in ditches at the side of the road. I struggled with two kitbags until the pain in my aching arms became unbearable, but I daren't put them down for fear of being unable to shoulder them again. However, I had reckoned without Tiny Bushell, who had seen my plight and come up behind me.

'Take a rest, Don,' he said quietly. 'I'll help you when you're ready.'

I fell back to the rear, but those few moments of respite enabled me to stagger on until a postern tower loomed into sight to tell me the ordeal was over. But now old fears returned.

In the misery I had almost forgotten the escape equipment secreted in one of my kitbags – that is until I saw the trestle tables lined up in an enclosure outside the main compound. They were waiting for us like customs officers eyeing the arrival of a party of tourists.

In the initial jostling and confusion, Sergeant Barnes managed to hide his contraband in some bushes, but I had no such opportunity and found myself pushed towards an oversized corporal.

'Warum zwei?' (Why two?) asked the searcher.

'I have been a prisoner a long time. One collects many things,' I replied in my best schoolboy German.

'Öffnen Sie das!' he ordered, pointing to the bag that contained nothing illegal.

I spread the contents on the table before him: dirty clothes, dirty sleeping bag, dirty dixie, dirty everything. My pulse beat out distress signals. The corporal screwed up his face in disgust, ignored the other kitbag and pushed me brusquely in the direction of the main gate of the compound. Had the escape equipment and false documents been discovered, I would have suffered the same fate as George Grimson at the hands of the Gestapo. I walked away quickly, feeling the hard steel of wire cutters biting into my left shoulder.

The committee was delighted with the return of the escape equipment – particularly the documents, which would have caused an uproar if they had been discovered. I was advised that information had come from the U.K. instructing prisoners not to risk their lives as the war was in its final stage. However, news about the defeat of our parachutists at Arnhem quickly put a damper on my optimism. I had dreams in which there was a stalemate in which neither side could break out for years and years. (The same dream still returns to me from time to time.)

I had heard that my brother Stewart was now an officer in the Parachute Regiment, and this news was now giving me concern for his safety – particularly when hundreds of forlorn young soldiers, wearing red berets, were marched into the camp. Their morale was at a low ebb and the crude tents in which they were billeted did nothing to raise it. I walked amongst them, seeking news of my brother, but I could find nobody who had knowledge of his fate.

The winter of 1944-45 seemed endless. The weather was bitter and our rations without food parcels were barely enough to sustain life. The barrack blocks were so crowded that what little cooking we could do became an impossibility, forcing most prisoners to squat outside with improvised heating devices made from tin cans in order to make a hot drink. The chief sources of fuel were waste paper and wood scrounged from any construction which could be vandalised without detection.

However, there was one consolation: a plentiful supply of books provided by the International Red Cross Society. Thus I was able at times to transcend the awfulness of my situation to enter the fictitious worlds of Walpole, Wells, Steinbeck, Galsworthy, Lewis and many others. Textbooks were also available and, with the help of a former schoolmaster, I brushed up my English, maths and history – hoping to reach university entrance level, if only to avoid returning to that soul-destroying task at the automatic Ladbroke telephone exchange.

Thoughts of escaping would not go away. They were quite logical, for although it was becoming increasingly clear that the war would end before another winter set in, deep down there was a nagging need to prove to myself that I could outwit my captors and restore some of my lost pride, in spite of the official warnings to keep inside the barbed wire.

With the aim of improving my spoken German, I made friends with an elderly guard who had seen service in the First World War and believed the present conflict was simply a return fixture. He was an ardent supporter of Hitler and, although he admitted that his side was suffering from severe setbacks, he was certain that his Führer would find a way. A secret weapon would erase London and bring victory to the homeland. All these hopes were recounted without any malice – in a soft southern accent – as if the outcome were an absolute certainty.

My colloquial German was soon making great strides, along with a small improvement in my meagre diet, for the guard seemed to have an inexhaustible supply of onions. A tap on the window near my bunk in the early hours was the signal to barter a few English cigarettes (the common currency of prison camps) for a haversack of onions. I soon became known throughout the compound as the King of the Zwiebels (King of the Onions), having cornered the market in this particular commodity.

In late January of 1945, instructions were received from the Red Cross that prisoners who so wished could sit the matriculation of London University. I decided to enter for the exam, realising that a chance had been presented which could provide me with a basic qualification that I had been unable to achieve during my curtailed schooling.

Huddled in a tatty greatcoat, I struggled with an essay on 'Freedom'. My brain cells didn't seem to appreciate the onion nutrients circulating in my sluggish blood, and they refused to solve quadratic equations or to divulge the correct order of Henry VIII's six wives.

It turned out that most of my effort was wasted, for only half of the papers reached England and I had to sit the bulk of them again after my repatriation. In later years, when seeking promotion, I was sometimes tempted to include in the application a reference to my academic training at the University of Stalag Luft III.

As the days lengthened, I noticed an unusual smell drifting over the camp when the wind was in the west. I questioned my guard about it but he shrugged his shoulders and walked away. My memory bank equated it with the smell I had once sniffed near a rope factory on the outskirts of Edinburgh. But now my nose detected a subtle difference – there seemed to be an element normally associated with cooking.

The mystery was not resolved until after the war, when I discovered that our camp lay to the east of Belsen, with its notorious gas chambers and incinerator ovens.

Fresh hope came with the spring. The Allies were advancing

again and the Russians were racing towards Berlin. Our secret wireless set was doing a wonderful job.

By the middle of March, an air of optimism pervaded the whole camp – an optimism that was shattered one morning when it was announced that the camp was to be evacuated within forty-eight hours. The destination was unknown, but it would obviously be in the opposite direction to the advancing British forces.

I decided to avoid the parties of two to three hundred which were being hurriedly assembled by the main gate as each barrack block was emptied in strict numerical order. I sought cover in one of the deserted huts and I managed to avoid detection for two days. Of course, I wasn't the only one practising this stratagem and the Germans soon got wise to it. They started searching the empty barracks and they threatened those they found with 'Hundstrafe', which literally translated means dog punishment. I only had a hazy notion of what this implied until the evening of the second day of the evacuation. I was lying under a palliasse on a top bunk in one of the forbidden huts when the door opened and two guards entered, both handling Alsatian dogs. I lay shaking with fear, expecting to hear at any moment a growl of triumph and to feel the pain of the hunters' teeth in my flesh. Although one guard came almost to the foot of the bunk, neither he nor his dog found me. It was midnight before my pulse returned to normal.

The following day, I decided not to chance my luck any further, so I joined the last party to leave the camp. I felt tired and ill as I waited to move off – the effects of under-nourishment and general deprivation had seriously weakened me and I doubted my physical ability to march more than a few miles.

To make the going easier, I had jettisoned most of my belongings and I started the march with only a few basic essentials carried in a small haversack.

The spring day brightened our way and brought us an unexpected warmth, which was not appreciated by the heavily laden guards in their winter greatcoats. The column was led by a fat Unteroffizier riding a bicycle, who zig-zagged along the rough track like a drunken circus performer. Every now and again, he dismounted to urge on his charges or to bark orders at the sweating guards strung out along each side of the column at intervals of about fifteen yards.

We passed a group of SS troops digging trenches across the road as it entered a forest. They seemed full of confidence and laughed amongst themselves.

'They are wasting their time,' I said to an elderly guard puffing alongside.

'Our Führer will find a way,' he replied.

The gravel road snaked through the forest, blotting out the sun and luring us to the freedom in the shadows of the trees.

Now we were allowed a five-minute rest – the Unteroffizier was finding it tough going. I found myself sharing a fallen tree with Paddy Dickson, a red-haired Irishman whom I had known since the first days of my captivity.

'I'm not staying with this lot,' he grunted.

I looked at him. His cheeks were sunken but his hair and particularly his eyes seemed to blaze with defiance.

'Why not?' I said.

'Because I'll not bloody well make it, that's why. I've no intention of finishing up with one of those bastards sticking a bayonet in me.'

'We'll make a run for it at the first opportunity,' I said. 'In the meantime, we mustn't get separated.'

Soon we were trudging up a rise where the road took a sharp turn to the right. Paddy grabbed my arm. 'Are you thinking what I'm thinking?' he said.

I nodded and looked behind. We were with the stragglers and there was only one guard, who would be out of sight for about two seconds once we had rounded the bend.

'Are you ready, then?' I said.

Paddy hesitated. 'Have you any matches?'

'No,' I answered.

'Pity, we could do with them, but it's too late now. I'm ready when you are.'

When the moment came, we charged into the forest like creatures stricken with blind panic. The trees were spread thinly and, at first, offered little cover. A carpet of dead leaves enveloped our feet of lead, but distant shouts spurred us on until our legs gave out and we both fell in a heap under the branches of a towering oak tree. We gasped for breath and, above the sound of our breathing, we heard the barking of dogs. We staggered to our feet and plunged a few more yards before collapsing in a shallow dell thick with young saplings. We lay there a long time, listening to the noise of the column dying away and watching intently for the signs of guards sent to pursue us.

Soon all was quiet and we seemed alone in a vast forest without food, without a map or compass and without any means of lighting a fire. At least we were free and filled with a sense of elation: the seriousness of our plight only became apparent with the approach of dusk.

We spent a sleepless night on a bed of damp leaves, and as soon as the first light filtered through the canopy of bare branches, we started walking briskly in what we hoped was a westerly direction.

By noon we were still in the forest and our pace had slackened to an aimless amble. The weakness I'd felt at the outset of the forced march had become noticeably worse, and Paddy seemed to be experiencing similar symptoms – wobbly legs and lightheadedness. Neither of us brought up the subject of food and water: our bodies kept reminding us of the need to take some positive action, but discussion seemed pointless. Where do you get food and water from in the middle of a nowhere forest?

Suddenly Paddy raised an arm. He was crouching a few yards ahead at the foot of a rise. I edged forward to join him.

'Look up there,' he whispered.

I looked and saw a pair of jackboots partially obscured by dense scrub. The sight filled me with alarm when I realised that the boots were occupied – they were moving slowly beyond the summit of the hill.

Paddy beckoned me to stay where I was and started to crawl upwards. I watched him reach the top and disappear from view. I lay still and all the forest seemed alive with enemy soldiers. I could see steel helmets behind every tree and bush. It was hopeless. I was completely surrounded. Any second now a shot would ring out and I would stand with my arms held high, waiting for the bullet which would make a mockery of this reckless attempt to escape. I waited an eternity – my body flattened to the earth – but nothing happened. I searched the trees on all sides, but I was alone with my fear. Had I experienced a hallucination? I didn't ponder it – there were more important things on my mind. Where the hell had Paddy got to? Why hadn't he come back down the hill?

It wasn't a difficult decision to make, for I couldn't survive on my own. I must go up the hill and find out what had happened to him. I'd almost reached the top when two figures rose from the ground and I felt myself lifted bodily over the ridge into a hollow on the other side. Paddy was sitting surrounded by a group of men wearing fur-trimmed helmets. Immediately I recognised the headgear worn by Russian soldiers.

I watched as a tall, gaunt fellow turned over the contents of my haversack, which was returned to me minus a pair of hand-knitted socks – a gift from my Great Aunt B.

This must be communism in practice, I thought, as I watched Paddy reluctantly surrender a woollen scarf and a large knife.

'Churchill, gut,' said the tall man, pulling my socks over feet wrapped in filthy pieces of rag.

'Churchill, gut,' chorused the watchers, beaming with friendliness.

'Stalin, gut,' I responded in an effort to encourage a much-needed relationship. Using a mixture of basic German and sign language, Paddy and I negotiated a deal: they would provide us with food and shelter and we would look after their interests when 'Churchill's soldiers' arrived. We shook hands with each comrade before squatting on the rim of the hollow to share a meal of jacket potatoes and rye bread.

There were ten of them – nine Russians and a Czech. Arkadie, a lieutenant tank commander, seemed to be the boss, but Wladimir had the same rank and sometimes challenged Arkadie's authority. Archip, Boris, Grigory, Jakow, Grigoril and another Wladimir were ordinary soldiers, and the Czech, whose name I cannot recall, never explained to me how he came to be hiding with a group of escaped Russian prisoners.

'How did you escape?' I asked.

In reply, fingers were drawn from ear to ear across several Russian throats. Yes, I decided, a close, friendly relationship with these men must be cultivated without delay.

Later in the day, we followed the group deeper into the forest until we came to a deep trench covered with branches and leaves. This was a communal sleeping place and, when night came, we all piled in to form a kind of human compost heap until we climbed out stiff and asphyxiated to gulp in the cold dawn air.

A dixie of steaming hot porridge soon put us in good heart and generated a lively discussion about the plans for the day ahead.

Paddy found that he could not stomach the coarse food, and I suspected that he was suffering from some kind of serious intestinal disorder. Every day he grew more listless and just sat under a tree, refusing to eat anything. Had the weather not been unseasonably mild, his condition would have worsened more rapidly. As it was, he became a constant source of concern to me and probably the Russians too, who saw their insurance policy becoming less effective.

Although the trench seemed to be well hidden, I was surprised to discover that it had been dug quite close to the road along which I had recently marched. During the second night, wedged between two slumbering Russians, I heard tracked vehicles rumbling close by. A convoy of German tanks – or were they British? – seemed to be moving east. I listened intently and heard orders being shouted in German. Was a last-ditch stand in the forest being planned?

The following morning the Russians seemed less pleased with the siting of their hideout and a new trench was dug further away from the road. I pointed to the almost new spades. 'Where from?' I asked.

'From farm,' replied Arkadie.

'And our food?'

'From farm. Tonight, we go again to the farm to get food. You come too.'

I got the impression that his reference to me was more of an order than an invitation. I didn't mind, for I felt under an obligation to share the risks which the group were undertaking.

Paddy was too ill to join the raiding party, so I went along as the sole British representative, keeping close to the comrades for fear of getting lost in the dark.

We squatted at the edge of the trees, looking at farm buildings across a ploughed field. A meeting was held in excited, unintelligible tones, and frequent references were made to 'the Englander', when heads were turned in my direction. It seemed that a special role had been devised for me – a role that was so secret and important that no one seemed ready to divulge it. One fact seemed certain: the Russians knew the layout of the farm – probably some of them had been employed there on a working party.

Soon we were scurrying across the furrows with backs bent below the moonlit horizon. Stealthily the Russians crept into the yard. I saw two enter the farmhouse by forcing a window: they returned seconds later to whisper that the farmer and his wife were sound asleep.

Now my particular part in the raid became apparent. A potato store had been located in a cellar under a barn, the door of which was padlocked. However, access could be gained down a chute normally used for filling the store. But these were not normal times and Grigory went down feet-first, followed closely by the British representative.

For several seconds I floundered about on a pile of potatoes, but when the darkness receded, I made out Grigory shovelling potatoes into a sack which I now grabbed to make his task easier. When it was almost full, I swung the load deftly on to my shoulder, surprised at its lightness. I groped about and discovered a large hole in the bottom!

Another sack was found and the operation was completed successfully in spite of a growing sense of claustrophobia, which threatened to unnerve me and send me rushing towards the only exit.

With the help of two comrades, the sack was eventually manhandled up the chute and Grigory departed in the same way with a little help from me to start him on his journey upwards. Then I jumped frantically up and down in my efforts to reach the bottom of the chute, which was about five feet above the potato pile. Fortunately, the watchers above quickly appreciated my plight and lowered a rescuer down by his feet to grab my outstretched arms and pull me to safety.

Soon all the loot was stacked out of sight on the edge of the field. Apart from the potatoes, there was a suckling pig, a churn of milk and several pounds of apples – enough to keep us all well fed for several days. I was about to suggest that it would be wise to gain the cover of the trees as soon as possible, when Arkadie said, 'There is another farm on the other side of the road.'

'You must be mad,' I said.

'More food, good, yes?'

'You are crazy, Arkadie.'

'More, good, very good.'

Keeping well to the rear, I followed the Russians out of the main gate towards another farm on the far side of a moonlit road. We were half-way across when a cyclist rounded the corner and almost collided with us. I saw at a glance he was a policeman.

The dark shapes in front exploded into the night and, for an instant, I was alone, held by the fleeting image of a uniformed figure swerving crazily towards a ditch. Now I fled back across the road towards the ploughed field and the safety of the trees beyond. Half-way across, I crouched in a furrow, gulping in the night air, and conscious that others close by were doing likewise. I heard distant, guttural voices complaining as, one by one, the farmhouse windows glowed pale yellow and the yard shone in the whiteness of a powerful arc lamp which, fortunately, did not illuminate the stack of stolen food at the edge of the field.

Soft whistles and hisses brought the comrades together. We squatted patiently, waiting for the lights to go out, then we gave the farmer and his wife about an hour to nod off, before creeping back to the scene of the crime.

We grabbed the food and scurried back to the forest – somehow I seemed to have been lumbered with the sack of potatoes, which impeded my progress considerably. In addition, I couldn't understand the sensation of some object scratching my back. I put the sack down and opened it to find a suckling pig trying to bite its way out! However, I was able to keep in touch with the others and, when almost within reach of the hideout, Boris offered to carry my load. I stubbornly refused to hand it over until the end of the journey, when it fell off my aching back and I slumped to the ground in a state of complete exhaustion.

Arkadie moved the milk churn close to where I lay. 'Guard it, comrade. It must not be touched,' he ordered, having removed the piglet.

I fell asleep where I had fallen and woke in the early hours to find my clothes soaked in dew. A figure rose from the ground and lifted the lid off the churn to scoop out some milk. I raised my head. The figure turned and whispered with a finger on his lips, 'Do not tell the others.'

The pantomime was repeated several times during the remainder of the night until every comrade had made sure of his milk ration. My understanding of communism in practice was proceeding apace.

Of course there were recriminations in the morning, and as the arguments raged, I took the opportunity to ensure that Paddy and I received our proper entitlement.

Regular nourishing meals were beginning to fill me out and generate the energy which I had lacked for so long. Paddy's health started to improve too, and he began to look less gaunt. Both of us relished the warm spring days which complemented the sense of exhilaration born on the wings of our new freedom.

Water was always a problem. There was a well or a spring – language barriers made it difficult to find out which – somewhere in the forest. One evening, the Czech and I were detailed to fill the water bottles. My companion, I was told, would lead us directly to the water, but after following him for two hours in the inky blackness, it became obvious that he was completely lost. After stumbling over countless fallen trees and crawling through dense undergrowth, I decided that enough was enough.

'I go no further,' I shouted.

He turned, shrugged his shoulders and disappeared from sight. I stood hesitating, not knowing which way to head. There was no moon to give shape to the black trees encircling me – only the high branches were visible standing out against a steel-grey sky. I had a gut feeling that the hideout lay to the east, but no such feeling told me in what direction to walk. Then I remembered that moss grows on the north side of tree trunks. I examined dozens of trees but I could find no trace of moss. In the end, I decided just to walk in a straight line and hope for the best. Eventually, I came to a narrow path which I followed for about a mile when I sensed some person or persons coming in the opposite direction towards me.

I stood behind a tree. A dog barked in the distance. The shuffling sounds ahead faded. I walked a few paces forward and stood behind another tree. Again the sounds rose and fell back. I waited, sensing that others were waiting too. The strain became intolerable. It would soon be daylight. I had to act without further delay. I stepped on to the track and called out in my best German, 'I'm a British prisoner of war. Who are you?'

The answering cry warmed my heart. 'Petrovitch! Petrovitch!' The comrades emerged from the darkness to embrace me like a long-lost prodigal son. Was their obvious relief an indication of their affection and concern for my safety? Or were they just happy to have retrieved the insurance they valued so much? Perhaps they were motivated by both considerations.

The Czech had found his way back, with empty bottles, to a critical and unfriendly reception – listening to the argument, I gathered that losing me in the forest was a bigger crime than not finding the water. Suddenly, I started to feel quite important.

The following evening, two comrades set out with the bottles again, to return before midnight with sufficient water to last us several days.

Sometimes, R.A.F. Typhoons would be seen screaming low

over the trees. They were an encouraging sight – particularly to the Russians, but when a week passed without any aerial activity the mood changed. 'Where is the English Luftwaffe, Comrade?'

I made optimistic replies but sometimes Arkadie's persistent questions would get on my nerves. 'Where are the English soldiers?' he would ask every morning.

'Where are the Russian soldiers?' I would counter, just to keep him in his place.

One evening, I set out with the comrades to find another group which, it was rumoured, were hiding up in the woods. After walking for half an hour, we saw a small clearing lit by a large camp fire around which several figures were seated. We walked boldly into the circle of light, causing some commotion until our identities were established.

The group seemed to consist mainly of Poles on the run from local slave labour camps. One middle-aged man, speaking in broken English, told me that he was the former chief of police in Warsaw before the German occupation. His wife and four children had been killed in an air raid.

What surprised me most in this encounter was the indifference which these men showed to the risks of having a large fire illuminating their presence. So unlike the comrades, who had impressed on me from the beginning how important it was to keep a low profile – voices down and careful, cat-like movements. Perhaps this lack of caution displayed by the Poles indicated a more up-to-date knowledge of troop movements than we possessed ourselves.

One morning, about two weeks after Paddy and I had first met up with the Russians, a great shout rose from the forest as if, simultaneously, droves of fugitives had found a long-sought-after sanctuary. It could mean only one thing – the Allied forces had arrived. Jakow rushed into the clearing.

'Churchill's soldiers are here – in the village – there is a tank

– others have seen it!'

He threw his cap into the air and danced a jig round me. The others gathered and lifted Paddy and me aloft as if we were personally responsible for arranging the arrival of the British forces.

We walked to the village, but there were no tanks to be seen. Tomorrow we would walk further west; in the meantime there was a bunkhouse where the comrades had slept when they had been employed as slave labourers on local farms.

The Poles had got there before us but there was still enough room. I chose a top bunk and soon drifted into sleep until my bladder started to complain in the early hours. No sooner had I placed a foot on the cold concrete floor than an escort appeared on each side.

'Where are you going, Petrovitch?'

'I'm going outside to have a piss.'

'We will go with you.'

Their trust in me was obviously under some strain.

Breakfast was being prepared when the door burst open and a policeman entered, waving a pistol. The Russians looked terrified and shrank away from the intruder. The Poles sat and looked disdainful.

'I'm a British prisoner of war. What do you want with us?'

'Farms have been plundered round here and I'm looking for the criminals.'

'We are looking for the British Army. We are soldiers, not criminals. Put your gun away, it may go off.'

The policeman saluted and left as suddenly as he had arrived.

Whilst waiting for the porridge to cook, Paddy and I strolled outside in the bright sunlight. We wandered westwards along the road, walking slowly as if uncertain of our motives. We rounded a bend and kept walking. Five miles later we were approaching the main gate of our former prison camp, watching the flags of Allied nations fluttering where once the Nazi flag had flown.

Tanks and lorries passed us, heading east along the road we had just taken. They were manned by cheerful, sun-tanned British soldiers – a welcome contrast to the grim faces of our former guards, now just visible beyond the barbed wire, standing to attention equipped only with buckets and brooms.

In the fields around, I could see the bloated bodies of horses and cows inflated by their own putrefaction; and in the far distance a spiral of smoke rose from a shattered farmstead to stain a cloudless blue sky. Obviously, the war had passed close to the Fallingsbostel camp.

I turned to grasp Paddy's hand and to look for the last time at the gaunt face, now alive with a new spirit. This was it. This really was the end, and I had survived almost five years of captivity. There had been times when I could see no end to the conflict, when in my worst dreams I was condemned to a life of imprisonment and slave labour. But now the sweet smell of freedom was in my nostrils: not a freedom tainted with the fear I'd felt in the forest hideout, but a safe freedom – a freedom guaranteed by my liberators, the men of the Tenth Armoured Division.

Then I remembered those who had saved our lives: Arkadie, Boris, Grigory and the others. We had made them a promise. They had looked after us, now it was our turn to keep our side of the bargain. It would be a long walk back and we were both tired and hungry.

'What are we going to do, Paddy?'

'I know what I'm going to do – I'm going in there to get a shower and a meal.'

'What about the Russians?'

'I don't care a damn about those dirty sods. We don't owe them anything.'

I hesitated. Paddy walked to the gate and spoke to the British sentry.

I knew what I had to do. I turned and walked back down the

road.

When I reached the bunkhouse I found the Russians despond-
ent and almost in tears.

'It's O.K. I'll take you to the camp. You'll have food and water
there. There is no need to worry. You start now. I'll catch you up.
I must have a little rest. See you outside the main gate.'

Only the Poles remained, sitting round a table in silence,
munching away at piles of freshly baked scones made from a
stolen sack of flour. I felt very hungry but I was too proud to ask
them for a share of their food.

After a short rest, I set off again along the road, determined to
overtake the comrades, who would probably get a cool reception
unless I was there to speak on their behalf.

I passed a cottage almost hidden by a tangle of scrub. I hadn't
noticed it on the earlier walk with Paddy, but now my senses had
alerted themselves to the possibility of food; so I swung round
and marched up to the back door, conscious of eyes watching me
from a shrubbery beyond a line of flapping clothes.

I entered a neat little kitchen with red gingham curtains and
a table in the centre covered with the same material. I knew
I was taking a risk but I was motivated more by hunger than reason. I doubted if there would be any serious opposition, for all
able-bodied men had long since been conscripted into the forces,
and womenfolk were unlikely to challenge a ravenous, bearded,
gaunt-faced refugee. Nevertheless, it was a strange feeling to be
poking about in someone's house, to see photographs on the side-
board of a young man in uniform, to see letters carefully stacked
behind a candlestick on the mantelpiece, to see a child's dress,
bristling with pins, laid on the arm of an easy chair. Suddenly
I felt a sense of shame. I snatched open a cupboard: it contained
cleaning materials, a box of matches and a packet of macaroni.
I left everything as I found it and hurried back to the road.

It was midday now. Dust rose to turn my mouth dry and cling

to the sweat on my face. Only in the shadows of the grass verge did the moisture linger; but death lingered here, too, in the shape of countless Panzerfaust anti-tank weapons jettisoned by those given the impossible role of making a last stand. I left them well alone, fearing that some might be booby-trapped.

Within a mile of the camp, I met up with a Canadian. We exchanged experiences. He had escaped from a working party and was heading for the same destination as I was. He'd only been a prisoner for nine months but he spoke bitterly about the treatment he had received.

'Came down over Hamburg. Some of the local citizens got me and strung me up to a lamppost – fortunately the Wehrmacht came along before they could tighten the noose – finished up at Fallingsbostel – did you know there are 10,000 food parcels stuck in a siding at Hanover and the bastards won't supply road transport …?'

The monologue stopped abruptly when a corpulent German soldier wobbled into sight over the brow of a hill, riding a bicycle laden with everything but the kitchen sink. There was a bulging suitcase strapped to the rear carrier, a vast amount of clothing and hardware attached to the crossbar and another case perched precariously on the handlebars. The man was unarmed and posed no threat to us.

The Canadian held up his hand and ordered the unfortunate to dismount. The puffy red face seemed to lose some of its colour and the chubby hands gripping the machine turned white at the knuckles.

'Ja, Ja,' he said between wheezes.

'Give me!' ordered the Canadian, pointing to the soldier's wristwatch.

The terrified man obeyed without protest.

'Is that necessary?' I asked, seeing the man's obvious distress.

'The bastards took my watch when I was shot down. I'm only returning the compliment. Give me!' ordered the Canadian, kicking the front wheel of the bicycle.

The German hesitated.

'Now!' shouted the Canadian.

One by one, each item of baggage was off-loaded until they were all stacked in a pile at the side of the road. Then the Canadian mounted the bicycle and rode away.

I often wonder what happened to the fat man. The last sight I had of him, he was sitting with his head in his hands, sobbing like some Germanic Billy Bunter. I wouldn't have been surprised if he had shouted after the Canadian, 'You dirty, rotten cad, I'll report you!'

I caught up with the comrades just before they reached the lager entrance. The sentry looked at us in astonishment.

'What have we got 'ere then?' said a sergeant major, emerging from the guard house.

'Warrant Officer Donaldson, 580770 and a small contingent of our noble Russian allies.'

'Where the hell have you come from?'

'I escaped from the march out of here. I've been living with these chaps in the forest for over two weeks.'

'You look as though you have just walked from Siberia.'

'Are you going to let us in, then?'

'I thought you lot had been ordered not to escape.'

'I thought it would be preferable to getting a bayonet up my backside.'

Finally, the gate was opened and, strange though it may seem, I walked with the comrades into my former prison camp – to freedom.

Two days later, my name was broadcast over the camp loudspeaker and I made my way to a convoy of British army trucks waiting to take us on the first part of our journey home. Suddenly a horse and cart came thundering across the compound in a cloud of dust. The comrades had come to see me off. They were all beaming with delight and offered the horse and cart as a parting gift.

'Where did you come by that?' I said.

'Farm near camp – very good food – very good horse – you take him back to England.'

There were handshakes all round. There were cheers for Churchill. I felt glad that I'd gone back.

Forty-eight hours later, I was looking down on the white cliffs of Dover from the cabin of a Dakota.

Had I not felt so ill with dysentery, I would have enjoyed the reception at R.A.F. Benson in Oxfordshire, which was both efficient and human-hearted. Every ex-prisoner of war was escorted from the aircraft by a young W.A.A.F. to a hangar which had been cleverly adapted to provide a range of facilities. After a hot meal and a shower, I was medically examined and later given a ration book endorsed with 'Malnutrition' – a magic word which entitled me to double rations.

I felt like a boy preparing for his first day at school as I dressed myself in new service clothing and sewed on my badges of rank. By nightfall, I was exhausted and crept between the first sheets I had known for many a year.

The following day, I received treatment for dysentery and congestion of the lungs. The medicine tasted foul but it seemed to do me a power of good and I felt well enough to participate in the next stage of my repatriation – a journey by R.A.F. transport to London for briefing and documentation.

Before leaving I had a good look round for Paddy, but I saw no sign of him: in fact, I never saw him again. I hoped earnestly that he made it back to Belfast all right.

In the early evening, as the truck rumbled through the villages, news had travelled ahead that ex-prisoners of war were passing through. I saw groups of people standing at the roadside, waving and cheering. Packets of sweets, bars of chocolate and cigarettes were thrown in our direction: it was a very moving experience.

In London, I was given a railway warrant, identity card, a month's pay and – perhaps the most treasured document of all – a pass authorising me to go on indefinite leave.

'It's Peter Donaldson, isn't it?'

The voice seemed familiar but I couldn't put a name to it.

'Remember me, D block at Sagan?'

I turned to scrutinise the face. 'You had a beard then. You look almost civilised now, Tom. Where are you heading for?'

'Brighton. Where are you going?'

'Shepperton. My mother has a cottage there.'

With large numbers of former aircrew being processed by the repatriation machine, it was inevitable that I would come across a former 'kriegie'. Now, as I sat in a station refreshment bar, I began to realise how much I had come to depend on the prison camp camaraderie. It was like meeting a compatriot in a remote foreign country.

I asked him about Paddy. He had heard nothing.

'What about Todd Hawkins – he was a great pal of mine?'

'Haven't you heard?' he replied.

Todd was on the second party to move out of Fallingbostel. The column was attacked by a low-flying Typhoon. Todd rushed from cover to display a hastily contrived P.O.W. sign. He was killed instantly. Poor Todd, I thought. He'd been a prisoner for five years, living only for the day when he would return to his wife and small son whom he had never seen. Fate had dealt him a losing hand – shot down on his first trip, made to suffer all the indignities of imprisonment only to be blown to pieces by a British cannon shell.

I had wired Mother to expect me about lunchtime. I walked from the station with my new kitbag on my shoulder: it felt lighter than the sack of potatoes I had carried only a week ago. As I neared the cottage, the door flew open and there was Mother, rushing out to meet me.

My young brother, John, hung back awkwardly. He was a tall, slender, good-looking teenager but almost a stranger.

Later my sister Jean joined us, looking very attractive in her A.T.S. uniform. The family reunion was only marred by the worrying news about Stewart – he had been reported missing after the Arnhem operation and our hopes were only temporarily restored when a fellow officer reported seeing him in a field hospital. Confirmation of his death was not received for several months after my return.

Life with Mother was not easy. She still had financial problems stemming from the complete cessation of Father's alimony. I was making a contribution and so was Jean, but our combined efforts were not enough to dispel the bitterness she felt towards Father and his cleverness in dodging a series of court orders. Of course, the constant uncertainty about Stewart didn't help matters.

I had Father's address so, at mother's behest, I travelled north to visit him in Cheadle, where he was living with his second wife and ten-year-old daughter. The meeting was an unmitigated disaster. I phoned him from a telephone kiosk outside the railway station. His wife answered. The conversation which followed went something like this:

'Hello, do you want to speak to my husband?'

'Yes, please.'

'I'm afraid he's in bed. He works at night, you know. Is it Mr Blank about the position in the estate agent?'

I mumbled something.

'He could be there by two o'clock.'

I mumbled again.

'I'll tell him. Good-bye.'

Return of a dearly beloved son. Prisoner of War Germany 1940 to 1945

'Good-bye.'

I'm not sure why I thought it necessary to act in this way. I certainly wanted to find out if my father was in, and probably I thought that he might have taken steps to avoid me if he had known I was on my way to visit him.

The second Mrs Donaldson came to the door of a tall, imposing Victorian residence. She didn't recognise me for I had seen neither her nor my father for over eleven years. She showed no surprise when I announced my name, but I detected a certain detachment in her manner, as if my intrusion was something to be tolerated rather than welcomed.

I stood in the hall looking at a young girl in a tartan skirt and realising suddenly that rumours about a 6-year-old half-sister were true.

'Peter is here to see you, Willy!'

'Peter who?' came the muffled query from upstairs.

'Peter Donaldson!'

There was a long pause and then the sound of carpet slippers on the landing before my father appeared, white-haired, pink-faced and somewhat ill at ease. We talked for a while in the sitting room, but I did not broach the subject of the financial plight of my mother.

'I'm afraid I have to go out. I've got an appointment about a job in a local estate agent's,' said my father.

'I'll walk down with you,' I said.

Once outside I put him in the picture. He was very disappointed as he saw no prospects in his present employment – a postal sorter on the night shift in Manchester. His standard of living was due largely to the income that his wife obtained from managing a private nursing home.

I broke the news about Stewart to him. He dabbed his eyes with a spotless handkerchief and then asked me if I had won any medals. I left him on the platform at Cheadle – a sad old man unable to command a good salary and unable to explain why he had never written to me during my imprisonment. I bade him farewell and never saw him again.

I had to get away from Shepperton, for my relationship with Mother was causing unbearable strain. She wanted me to mix freely with her friends in the local pub, but I found myself shrinking from the loud voices and trite opinions.

Perhaps the authorities could have done more to prepare families on how to best deal with returning prisoners of war. Many, including myself, found adjustment difficult; others, even less fortunate, suffered mental disorders which sometimes led to prolonged illness or even suicide.

(I recall once, during a particularly harsh time, saying – almost intuitively – to a fellow prisoner, 'Perhaps, one day, some of us will wish we were back behind the barbed wire.' It was a stupid remark and deserved the scorn it received. Yet it contained a grain of truth, for I heard later that two prisoners of war who had formed a homosexual relationship both took their own lives after returning to England.)

The only friends I had were now dispersed throughout the land – apart from those who befriended me and my fellow airmen in the Yorkshire town of Ripon. I would go north to seek them out.

Mallorie Park Drive, on the outskirts of the town, had a row of modern houses at its northern end. One of these was the home of a family which had shown great kindness to members of the forces. They owned the local cinema and always reserved a few seats at the back for friends of the family, among whom I counted myself.

Thelma came to the door. 'Peter!' she exclaimed, her lean, angular face a picture of surprise.

'Thought I'd look you up, Thelma,' I said as if it were still 1940 and I'd just slipped out of Dishforth between raids.

I walked in, half expecting to see Walter Coveney and Jack Davis chatting to Granny Wood, but the old lady sat stiffly in a chair, crippled with arthritis, staring in front of her as if she were sharing my dreams.

I learned later that I had caused quite a panic, for Thelma was engaged to the Chief Medical Officer at the local army camp, and I was probably the last person she wanted on her doorstep. She made a hasty telephone call to a young lady friend lodging nearby. Nancy Knowles was not pleased to be landed with an unknown airman, for she had other plans for the evening ahead; but Thelma begged, and Nancy, perhaps out of curiosity, gave in and came round to meet me.

I suppose it was love at first sight. Nancy was tall, slender and very attractive. She had beautiful blue eyes set in a strong face, and there was an aura of generosity and compassion about her which touched a long-forgotten need deep within me. She searched my face and I got the impression that she liked what she saw. Later that day, I borrowed a bicycle and joined both the girls for a trip into the country. I felt ecstatic. The weather was perfect, and here I was with two beautiful companions on a journey through a green, sunlit landscape – and not a barbed-wire fence in sight. This was freedom. For this I had struggled and survived.

In spite of Mother's strong disapproval, I married Nancy in Ripon Cathedral on September 19th 1945. Arthur, Thelma's brother, was my best man. A honeymoon in Edinburgh and Aberdeen followed before a posting to R.A.F. Madley near Hereford.

Germany and Japan had been forced to accept unconditional surrender, and the expected high casualties amongst aircrew had never materialised: pilots and navigators were sweeping hangar floors or rushing to get demobilised. My career prospects looked poor, so with a view to enhancing them, I applied for a course in advanced navigation. The posting confirmed my suspicions

Author and Nancy on their wedding day posing outside Ripon Cathedral

Wedding day September 19 1945

– of twenty ex-P.O.W.s who attended the rehabilitation course, all were sent to Madley as motor transport mechanics under training.

I received permission to 'live out' and found a comfortable lodging with Elsie, a generous-hearted Welsh lady who introduced Nancy to her black market contacts, enabling her to cook meals which, up to that time, had only existed in my imagination.

The C.O. agreed that I wasn't cut out to be a motor mechanic and sent me to assist the Station Education Officer to run courses in vocational training. It was a simple case of the blind leading the blind as I became more and more involved in a variety of lectures, always struggling to keep a chapter or two ahead of my students.

The frequent absence of the Education Officer made matters worse. He had discovered a simple device for being with his family for most of every week: a weekend pass that was valid from Thursday morning until the following Tuesday afternoon. It carried his own signature and I seemed to be the only person on the station who knew what was going on.

It was suggested by a Senior Education Officer that I should be promoted to Flight Lieutenant and take charge of the Station Education Section. I was informed this would be expedited. This meant that the present Education Officer would have to work under my control. I learnt later that he wrote an unfavourable report on my abilities to prevent my promotion. Nice chap, wasn't he!

One day, I was summoned to an interview with the Commanding Officer.

'You were a prisoner of war, weren't you, Donaldson?'

'Yes, sir.'

'Well, I've got a job for you. I want you to go to a clearing station and escort about a hundred Jerries to Madley. We've been allocated them for a variety of jobs around the camp. The adjutant will give you all the details.'

'Will I get any assistance, sir?'

'Take a couple of airmen with you, Donaldson.'

'Thank you, sir.'

'Anything else?'

'Where will the Germans be billeted, sir?'

'I've arranged for a small compound to be fenced off round those empty barrack blocks to the north of the camp.'

'Who will be in charge of them, sir?'

'You will, Donaldson.'

'Thank you, sir.'

'Now, get on your way.'

The Germans were duly collected and transported to Hereford – not by cattle truck but in a specially reserved railway coach. The airmen and I patrolled the corridors, aware that our service revolvers were causing some amusement amongst our charges, for it was obvious that escape was far from their minds. They knew that they would be better fed and housed in England than in their devastated homeland.

As soon as I got them into the compound, the C.O. came striding in for an inspection. He was a large, bluff man with a prominent moustache.

'You speak German, don't you, Donaldson?'

'Well ... er ... a little, sir.'

'Tell them to form up in threes, right dress and then march in column of route to ...'

'I don't think I can quite manage that, sir,' I interrupted.

A young, fresh-faced German stepped forward to ease my predicament. 'I speak English,' he said in a cultured, upper-class accent.

Hans became my right-hand man, enabling me to establish an efficient administration, providing labour on request for every section of this large R.A.F. station. He explained how his compatriots had been captured by the Americans and then transported to prison camps across the Atlantic. Following the German surrender, it was announced that all prisoners would be repatriated, and within a few weeks they were travelling east in troopships. Imagine the dismay aboard Hans's ship when it was diverted to Southampton, where the prisoners disembarked to be transferred to British camps.

The Germans had been categorised into three divisions – black, grey and white – according to whether they were Nazis, non-Nazis or anti-Nazis. It seemed that the Madley inmates contained elements of all three.

One day Hans came to me in obvious distress. 'There has been trouble,' he said. 'Several Nazis have beaten up prisoners for listening to the B.B.C. news. They say it is all propaganda. I think you must take action or there will be more trouble.'

Hans gave me the names of the Nazis, so I phoned the adjutant for instructions. He told me to bring the offenders to the C.O.'s office at once.

Escorted by two redcaps and an Alsatian, the four prisoners were lined up in the corridor at the S.H.Q. whilst I went in to confer with the C.O.

The moustache bristled with determination. 'What is the charge, Donaldson?'

'Well, sir, if they're guilty I think—'

'Guilty? Of course they're guilty, man.'

'What about intimidation, then, sir?' I suggested, feeling somewhat intimidated myself.

The C.O. rose from his desk and climbed a small stepladder to reach a top shelf and take down a thick, dust-laden volume.

'Intimidation, you said … um … um. No mention of it here. I think we'd better settle for mutiny.'

'You can't do that, sir.'

'Why not?'

'Well, they're not subjects of the Crown,' I replied, trying to suppress the triumph in my voice.

'Right, send them in – we'll think of something.'

The four were subjected to a tirade which would have done justice to Adolf himself. Of course, the Germans had not understood a word and they were probably glad to reach the peace of the police cells, where they remained for a week. I never discovered the details of the charge – if there was any charge at all. However, Hans had a simple remedy for any Nazis who stepped out of line: he allocated them duties emptying latrine buckets.

About this time, I was summoned to the War Office to appear before a certain Major Browning, who wished to investigate my escapes and attempted escapes with a view to recommending me for a decoration.

I travelled to London and found the gentleman in a small office off Regent Street. He was young, fresh-faced, and spoke with a nasal drawl as if unsealing his lips would be contrary to the best traditions of the Intelligence Service. He asked me about my escapes with an air of disinterestedness, as if he had already decided not to issue any more gongs that day.

I rambled on for a few minutes but it all seemed a waste of time, particularly when he prompted me for details which I could not recall.

'It seems, Warrant Officer, that all your escapes were poorly prepared and had little chance of success. Your decision to make a bolt for it in the forests near Hanover was foolhardy, to say the least, as the war in Europe was almost at an end.'

Suddenly a wave of anger swept away my deference for his commissioned status. What the hell did he know about hunger and cold and despair? He'd probably spent the war behind a desk.

I rose abruptly, gave him a slow cynical salute, and walked out to join the throng in Regent Street celebrating V.E. day (Victory in Europe).

Presentation of Whitley Painting to senior officers at RAF Leeming

From: Group Captain J A Cliffe OBE FRAeS RAF

Royal Air Force
Leeming
Northallerton
North Yorkshire
DL7 9NJ

BT: (01677) 423041 Ext 7202
Fax: (01677) 423041 Ext 7033

LEEM/CO/4

Mr P Donaldson
7 Mallorie Close
RIPON
North Yorkshire
HG4 2QE

16 July 1999

Dear Peter

Unfortunately, I missed your presentation last Tuesday evening to the Leeming Branch of the Royal Aeronautical Society (I was delivering a Tornado to one of our squadrons which is currently deployed in Saudi Arabia). From what I have been told, I missed a most fascinating evening. I have just seen the portrait of the Armstrong Whitworth Whitley which you presented to my OC Engineering and Supply Wing, Wing Commander Chris Green. It is a wonderful picture, reflecting so much of the great history of RAF Leeming. I will ensure that it takes pride of place in our new station history room, and that the historic details of your fateful first mission from Leeming are appropriately recorded alongside.

I sincerely hope that you can return to Leeming for another presentation, for I would very much like to meet you and hear some of your recollections of flying from Dishforth and Leeming. The missions in which you were involved were truly heroic in every sense, helping to maintain the momentum of the war effort, and in keeping with the highest professionalism and spirit associated with the Royal Air Force to this day. On behalf of the Leeming Branch of the Royal Aeronautical Society, I thank you for finding time to come and talk to its members, and from all at RAF Leeming, very many thanks for your most kind presentation of the Whitley portrait.

sincerely

John

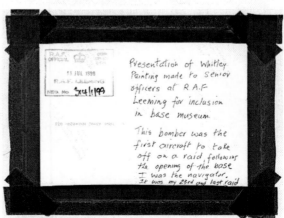

Presentation of Whitley Painting made to Senior officers at R.A.F Leeming for inclusion in base museum.

This bomber was the first aircraft to take off on a raid following the opening of the base. I was the navigator. It was my 23rd and last raid

APPENDIX A

RANKS AND BADGES

The term *observer* was a legacy from the Royal Flying Corps operating in biplanes during the First World War.

Most planes had two cockpits: the front one for the pilot and the rear one for the observer who navigated and manned the rear gun. The title 'observer' was still being used when the Second World War broke out, but later, navigation, bomb-aiming, gunnery, signals etc. were allocated to different individuals, all of whom were either commissioned officers or N.C.O.s.

Pilots' 'wings' have remained almost unchanged.

It is interesting to note the ranks of the aircrew of which I was a member when I was shot down.

Captain: Flight Lieutenant
2nd Pilot: Pilot Officer
Navigator: (That's me) Sergeant,
                    later promoted to Warrant Officer
Wireless Operator: Corporal.
Rear Gunner: Aircraftman

Nowadays, most members of an aircrew hold a commission.

I could display my observer's badge and the three chevrons, indicating the rank of sergeant. In fact, we were not supposed to display the former badge until we had completed a six-month probationary period on a squadron. Most observers ignored this regulation.

Badges modified in 1942
OBSERVER
NAVIGATOR
BOMB AIMER
WIRELESS OPERATOR
AIR GUNNER

APPENDIX B

OPERATIONS FLOWN

Operations Dates	Action	Flying Times
17/12/39	Dropping leaflets over Germany	6hr 40m
19/3/40	Bombing German mine laying Base on Island of Sylt	6hr 40m
20/4/40	Raid on Stavanger air base (diverted to Leuchars due to fog on return flight)	+ 1hr 55m
23/4/40	Raid on Aalsburg. Crashed landing on return	9hr 15m
1/5/40	Repeat raid on Stavanger	7hr 30m
15/5/40	Industrial targets in Ruhr, aircraft damaged by flak	8hr 15m
17/5/40	Bremen	7hr 40m
21/5/40	Low level attack on road & rail communications near Hirson	5hr 55m

24/5/40	Industrial targets in Ruhr Bomb hang-up	6hr 5m
25/5/40	Raid on oil targets	7hr 35m
27/5/40	Entered fierce magnetic storm. Read about the outcome in separate Report	8hr
3/6/40	Raid on Industrial targets In Rhur Valley	6hr 30m
5/6/40	Attacked German air bases in France	6hr 20m
6/6/40	Raid on marshalling yard aborted Captain sick – Returned to base	1hr 45m
11/6/40	Amiens Air base	6hr 40m
17/6/40	Low level bombing using the new W mine over Rhine near Mannheim (See main MSS & Appendix 3)	8hr 45m
18/6/40	Marshalling Yards near (Schwedt) Heavy flak – Rear gunner wounded	6hr 45m
20/6/40	Raid on Hamm Attacked by night fighter	7hr
21/6/40	Target Oil Plant at Salzbergen	6hr 40m
8/7/40	Klel Naval base under 10/10th cloud. Unable to bomb – shot down near Heligoland. Crew Taken P.O.W.	7hr 30m

If the dates of the above operations are studied, it becomes evident that many aircrews were not given sufficient rest between flights. Night operations lasted six, seven or eight hours. Additional time for briefing and debriefing meant that sheer lack of sleep was the cause of many accidents.

APPENDIX C

BOMBER COMMAND BY MAX HASTINGS

I had a phone call from Max, asking if he could come to the Russell School in Chorleywood to interview me. He was writing the above book and wanted information from a former bomber crew member who had been in the front line in the early days of the war.

He used all my information and I was honoured to see the very young Peter Donaldson pictured in his book.

APPENDIX D

THE W MINE

An extract from the Air Historical Branch states:

'The W bomb is an example of a weapon conceived in great haste and developed so rapidly that weak points in its design were inevitable. Its outstanding disadvantage lay in the fact that it could not be stored. Small batteries and soluble plugs deteriorated rapidly and were intended for immediate use. It was never completely safe. When the safety plugs hit the water they dissolved and the bomb became live. It floated just under the surface of the river and exploded when a boat passed over. It was intended for oil barges on the Rhine.

Following a heavy rainfall at Dishforth, two airmen were killed and three injured when a W bomb was being defused. Subsequently the bombs were withdrawn from use.'

APPENDIX E

THE CANCELLED RAID

There is no record of this raid in my logbook, so I am unable to provide an exact date. I recall the weather was warm, so I expect it occurred in late spring, 1940. I received a message from 'Crack 'Em' informing me that he had permission to make one final raid. The target chosen was a German battleship anchored in a Norwegian fjord. We planned to go in at low level and drop a flare, followed by a stick of bombs. We were taxiing on the tarmac, ready for take-off, when the raid was cancelled.

The Wing Commander stormed out of the aircraft, turned to me and said, 'I'm going to the mess to get drunk!'

I replied, 'I'm going to my billet to thank my guardian angel for this reprieve.'

APPENDIX F

PRISONER-OF-WAR CAMPS IN WHICH I WAS INCARCERATED

Dates	Camp – region	Notes
July 11th 1940 Several days	Dulag Luft, Frankfurt	Interrogation Centre
July 15th 1940	Stalag Luft 1, Barth	Escaped with Sergeant Stamford. Recaptured.
June 1941	Stalag VIII B, Lamsdorf	Known for its harsh conditions. Used as a punishment centre for R.A.F. escapees.
? 1942	Stalag Luft VI, Heydekrug	Near Königsberg on shore of E. Baltic.
? 1943	Stalag 357, Thorn, Poland	Attempted escape foiled.
? 1944	Stalag Luft III, Sagan, N.W. Breslan	This is the famous camp where a mass break-out occurred. Fifty officers were shot on order of Hitler.
? 1945	Stalag X1B, Fallingsbostel	I escaped from a forced march.

(Exact dates not remembered)